When Writers Read

Second Edition

When Writers Read
Second Edition

Jane Hansen
University of Virginia

Heinemann
Portsmouth, NH

Heinemann
A division of Reed Elsevier Inc.
361 Hanover Street
Portsmouth, NH 03801–3912
www.heinemann.com

Offices and agents throughout the world

The author and publisher wish to thank those who have generously given permission to reprint borrowed material:

Excerpt from **Barefoot Heart: Stories of a Migrant Child** (1999) by Elva Treviño Hart is reprinted by permission of Bilingual Press/Editorial Bilingüe, Arizona State University, Tempe, AZ.

Figures 12-1, 12-2, 12-3, and 12-4 first appeared in "Student Record Keeping" by Jane Hansen in **School Talk**. Copyright © 1997 by the National Council of Teachers of English. Reprinted with permission.

Library of Congress Cataloging-in-Publication Data
Hansen, Jane.
    When writers read / Jane Hansen.—2nd ed.
      p.   cm.
    Includes bibliographical references and index.
    ISBN 0-325-00300-9 (pbk.)
    1. Reading (Elementary)—United States. 2. Language arts—United States. 3. Education—United States—Experimental methods. I. Title.

   LB1573 .H1754 2001
   372.4—dc21   00-054068

Editor: Danny Miller
Production: Abigail M. Heim
Cover design: Jenny Jensen Greenleaf, Greenleaf Illustration and Design
Manufacturing: Steve Bernier

Printed in the United States of America on acid-free paper

05   04   03   02   01   VP   1   2   3   4   5

I dedicate this book

to

D. Graves

and

T. Newkirk

These two colleagues at the University of New
Hampshire pushed me the farthest.

Thank you.

Contents

Acknowledgments

This book covers many years of time and includes many people with whom I have laughed, worked, questioned, and agreed. It was much fun to relive many meetings and stories as I sat at my little laptop this year to write.

I begin by reacknowledging the teachers at the Mast Way School in Lee, New Hampshire. During recent years they have continued to offer their classrooms to me, as they did years ago before I wrote the original edition of this book in 1987. I feel so comfortable in their school. Some of them now teach in other schools, and I continue to learn from them.

I wrote here about the teachers at Stratham, the first school I researched in after my years at Mast Way. At Stratham I learned mainly in the library with librarians Betty Bachelder and Lucinda Wigode, but I walked in and out of classrooms to observe at will. Some of those teachers also teach elsewhere now, and I continue my contacts with them.

During those years, I appreciated these University of New Hampshire colleagues: Don Graves, Bill Wansart, Judy Fueyo, Ruth Hubbard, Brenda Power, Peggy Murray, Mary Ellen MacMillan, Mary Chase, and Ann Vibert.

Then, to Manchester, where I researched with many teachers, and here I thank those in the elementary schools of Wilson, Bakersville, and Beech, and especially thank Karen Boettcher, who was my partner for my first two years there.

These UNH colleagues studied with me during our years in that city: Bill Wansart, Don Graves, Cindy Matthews, Carol Wilcox, Danling Fu, Kathy Simons, Andrea Luna, Lisa Bianchi,

Doug Kaufman, Pat Aichele, Julie Brooks, Carol Hawkins, and Patty Hicks. I thank all for their stories and am very aware of those I didn't tell within these pages. If this book were as long as some of their dissertations, I could have included every single research anecdote.

I also wrote about teachers I know from my own teaching. It is in my own classes that I put into practice what I learn in schools, and it is these teachers who question me most carefully. They keep our profession alive and are determined to not stand still.

Elizabeth Lane was my wonderful secretary. She knows how much I hate to look for missing information and—even though I think she hates to search as much as I do—she can find anything I need in our voluminous files, bookshelves, stacks, and bottom drawers.

Thank you to Professor Francisco Cavalcante, Jr. for editing the first press pages of this book.

I close with thanks to Danny Miller, my new and very supportive editor. Thank you for your suggestions in green ink. This book has much space for marginal notes. I hope every reader keeps it alive with many thoughts in green—or my favorite, purple—ink.

When Writers Read They Evaluate

I begin with a test. In order to pass, you must not evaluate my mother, my dad, my self, nor me as a writer when you read the following passage. Please read:

> In the fifties I lived on a farm in southern Minnesota, in the same house my dad had lived in since he was a young teen, and he and Mother lived there until she died in 1998. Dad still lives there. For more than fifty years, that same farm and same kitchen table have been home. In that space I gradually learned to be myself, but my appreciation of the farm was slow to come. I may now nearly feel the devotion to it that my father feels. An only child, he lived on this farm with his ma and pa until his pa's death when my dad was twenty-five. Later that same year he married my mother. . . .
>
> When Mother was hospitalized for my birth he brought flowers, recorded for posterity in the remembrances my mother penciled on 2" × 3" sheets from the orange section of a small, rainbow tablet:
>
> *Wednesday night—Harry here. Brought flowers from home. Iris, poppies, lily of the valley. . . .*
>
> Mother gave me her memories from her ten hospital days, one sheet per day, on my fortieth birthday, a wonderful surprise. I didn't know they existed. She wrote about the struggles I, her firstborn, and she, a new mother, experienced, as the two of us struggled to adapt. . . .
>
> Jane Hansen, 1999
> *Ordinary Lessons: Girlhoods of the 1950s*

I assume you failed this test. In some way you evaluated either my mother, my dad, me, or me as a writer. You may have thought, "How wonderful," when you learned that my mother gave me her journal of my birth for my fortieth birthday. You may have thought, "How tragic," when you learned that my dad's pa died when my dad was only twenty-five. *When writers read,* they evaluate all the time. They can't help it.

Importantly, they can become better at it, and that is what this book is about: what students do to become better evaluators of themselves as readers and writers and what teachers do to help.

This book is called *When writers read* because my understanding of reading came when I studied writers. *When writers read,* they evaluate differently than nonwriters do. This begins when we reread our own work. When I read the previous passage, I think about my mother's gift to me and remember the scene in my sister's living room when she presented me with the little white envelope in which her journal had lived for forty years and the quilt she had made to accompany it. But, I decided to not write about the quilt because that might lead readers away from my focus on the journal.

When I read the line about the death of my dad's pa, I remember the news clip I found decades after his death. I had never known the cause of his death until that moment. As I read the news article, my dad sat six feet away on his dining room couch, watching TV. I felt dumbfounded by the tragedy I was reading and said, "I'm reading about grandpa's accident."

"Yeah, it was pretty awful." That's all he said. But I decided to not write those details, because I was writing about my mother's journal.

When writers read their own work, they realize how much their readers don't know. Later, when they read something written by another writer, they know how much is missing and wonder about the decisions that writer made. *When writers read,* they ask multitudes of questions and feel a sense of appreciation for the many decisions the writer made.

As soon as I published my original *When Writers Read* in 1987, I knew I had barely begun to understand the immensity of what writers do when they read. I decided, along with my co-researchers, to continue to research reading and writing, but in a different school and with a focus on evaluation. Why? Because evaluation practices in our profession were at odds with the effective writing and reading instruction I had just written about. Often, reports about a student's achievement did not include the student's viewpoint even though successful writing and reading instruction promotes strong student voices.

Also, the heart of writing and reading instruction rests on the evaluation process that lies at the heart of the teacher-student writing conference, regardless of whether individual conferences themselves are a central component of a particular teacher's classroom. In writing conferences, the main task of the teacher is to find out what excites the writer, to learn about that, and to find out from the student what is not going well. Thus, the student's task is to evaluate himself. The teacher responds with instruction based on the student's evaluation. This important role of the student-as-evaluator appeared to need clarification; without it, literacy instruction would be misguided.

So, along with a team of colleagues, I spent two days a week for three years in the Stratham Memorial School, the elementary school in Stratham, New Hampshire. A few years before we arrived, the teachers had created writing workshops that clicked. The children, for the most part, loved to write, and could.

Reading turned out to be another story. I sensed dissatisfaction on the students' part and interviewed several of them. Their words scared the principal (Hansen 1998b). The children didn't think they learned to read in school; they thought they learned to read at home. After taking some time to think about this, the principal talked to the teachers. They decided to visit Mast Way School, the school I wrote about in my first edition of *When Writers Read.* After some big changes, the Stratham children began to consider themselves both writers and readers—in school.

Throughout all of this, my reason for being at Stratham was to learn about what the students did as evaluators when they wrote and read. Initially, they evaluated themselves as writers in order to produce drafts that they, their classmates, and their teachers appreciated. However, they didn't evaluate what they read through that same lens. They weren't excited about what they read in reading class, didn't appreciate it, and didn't wonder about the decisions those writers made.

When these children started to read high-quality literature, they not only appreciated it but also mined that print for ideas for their own writing. They found topics they could write about and borrowed authors' ways with words. By consciously evaluating what they read, these young writers and readers became increasingly aware of what they could do and of what all writers and readers could do.

Much of this was new to me. I hadn't thought of evaluation as the search for processes that work. In Chapter Two of this book I write about what *e-value-ation* does to bring writing and reading together.

Whereas evaluation in Stratham was exciting, a new population challenged me. Jane Kearns, the writing coordinator of Manchester, the largest city in New Hampshire, invited me to bring a team of researchers to the urban schools of her beloved city. This is where my eyes widened. Years earlier I had taught in an urban school in Minneapolis and had become quite immersed in that community. Manchester provided a similar setting, but I was in for many surprises. The topics and techniques these students valued were much different from those I knew of in former days in Minneapolis and different from the current interests of the children in Stratham.

In Manchester the teachers invited their students to create portfolios to help them evaluate their writing, reading, and, as it turned out, themselves. Because of them, I started to place supreme importance on the power of voice. These students wanted to be heard. Thus, the next chapter of this book is titled "Voices," and is the first of my five core chapters: "Voices," "Decisions," "Time," "Response," and "Self-Discipline."

Reading and writing can't thrive unless our evaluation system honors a diversity of "Voices," the hallmark of writers. No two writers sound alike. Stephen King and Toni Morrison don't need their names on the covers of their books. If I were reading one right now, I wouldn't need to read far before I would know, for sure, which one authored the book in front of me. An effective evaluation system seeks, values, and promotes the individual voices of writers and readers.

In my previous edition of *When Writers Read,* I referred to the concept of *voices* in my chapter titled "Community." Now, not only am I tired of the word *community*, but I feel that *voices* is the concept within a community that shows the importance of it. A vibrant community is a collection of people with different voices who possess the self-discipline they need to find ways to value one another. Rather than compete to see who is better, these students seek to learn from various writers and readers. They reject elitism and embrace egalitarianism. No one is in a group designated as better than another. When all voices honor all voices, supported by an evaluation system dedicated to the notion that all students can stand tall, the classroom has a strong reading-writing program.

"Decisions" became my new title for my 1987 chapter "Choice." Decisions captures the notion behind choice. In the process of making choices, students evaluate a range of available options and make appropriate decisions. Writers and readers know why they choose certain types of writing, the topics they want to write about, where to work, specific times to do so, particular peers with whom to share, and specific persons to help them.

I kept "Time." It pervades all. The first thing the teachers I write about do when they plan for their teaching is create the overall framework in which their students will spend their time. Writers and readers write and read in school, in a workshop format, so their teachers and peers can be available to help them evaluate their work and provide assistance while they are in the process of writing and reading.

"Response" remains. It's the core of these five chapters. It's the center of the classroom in which writers and readers make wise decisions about what they want to write and read. An effective response system supports the writers and readers; it creates, maintains, and energizes their desire to learn. This response is the heart of the evaluation system. When an evaluation system begets the kinds of response writers and readers crave, the teacher and students are on track.

"Self-Discipline" is my new title for my old "Structure" chapter. *Structure* refers to the predictable schedules teachers create so their students know what to expect, when they will write and read next. They can plan ahead and be ready to go. Their own *self-discipline* keeps them engaged. It's helpful to them to receive response that urges them onward, but the test of this response is whether it fosters an internal drive. Writers and readers don't need teachers to nag them or motivate them. These students are motivated by the writing of professionals, the writing of their classmates, and their own work. Their heart-held belief in the importance of writing and reading gets them through tough times. Good books and writing possibilities find them ready to imbibe and self-disciplined enough to wisely use their time for these tasks they value.

This book is about what students who find value in themselves and others do when they read and write. They read and write differently from persons who don't care or who feel negatively toward themselves and others. They know their classmates and themselves as persons with histories, lives, and desires beyond school. Their teachers strive to help them appreciate and maintain the benefits their total selves give to their reader-writer selves.

Evaluation, | Two
E-value-ation

When Marguerite, a sixth-grade writer, looked for a book to read, she found *Oh, No, Toto!* (Tchana & Pami 1997), and loved the cover. Toto, a toddler, stands on a high box and snitches an egg from the tray of hard-boiled eggs the egg boy balances on his head as he walks through a village market in Cameroon. Marguerite imagined Toto's upcoming fall and opened the book to find out what happens to him. Simultaneously she thought of the cover for the book she was writing for the public library about the local farmers market and wondered what would attract readers' eyes.

When writers read, they continuously evaluate. In Marguerite's case, she found value in the work of other writers and illustrators. For her, to evaluate was to find value in something. Whereas writers may also find features they don't appreciate within the writing they read, their main approach to the work of other writers is one of appreciation and resourcefulness. When writers read, they look for useful ideas.

Rather than study the illustrations, a different reader of *Oh, No, Toto!* may evaluate the writers. "These two authors sure know lots about Cameroon. Do they live there?" According to the jacket, one author was a Peace Corps volunteer in Cameroon and the other is her sister-in-law, a Cameroonian. They have credibility.

Or, rather than evaluate the writers, readers may evaluate themselves as readers. When Darby, a second-grade child, chose to read this same picture book, she hesitated on the page that begins, "Quicker than lightning. . . ." She had never heard anyone say this and these words confused her. Darby walked over to her friend, who didn't understand either but loved the picture on this page and was instantly interested in this book. She convinced Darby not to worry about the troublesome words until later, and the two sat down to finish this book together. As they did so, they continuously evaluated, and their evaluations kept them engaged.

Voices

This week I attended an event at a local bookstore and heard Elva Treviño Hart read from her recently published memoir, *Barefoot Heart: Stories of a Migrant Child* (1999). I had read the book non-stop the previous day and had not yet recovered when Elva read. This book is powerful. Elva's soft voice surprised me as she began:

> I am nobody. And my story is the same as a million others. Poor Mexican American. Female child. We all look alike: dirty feet, brown skin, downcast eyes.
>
> You have seen us if you have driven through south Texas on the way to Mexico. We are there—walking barefoot by the side of the road. During harvest time there are fewer of us—we are with our families in the fields.
>
> Some of us grow up and move to cities. We work downtown and speak perfect English. Others of us stay. I don't know which is better.
>
> Sometimes we move to places where people don't know that underneath the wool crepe suit is a brown, barefoot little girl like me. Behind the university-speak is a whole magic world in Spanish. We play the game well and it looks as if we are happy. Sure, we're happy.
>
> But then, when we're flipping through radio stations on the way to the office, we get to the Mexican station, and they're playing our favorite corrido. It makes us long for mamacita, for tortillas, for the comadres and the tias, for dancing rancheras in the hot, sweaty night under the stars at the fiesta.
>
> Then the nine-to-five life seems dry as a stone and without a soul.
>
> "How did I get here?" we ask.
>
> I'll tell you.

Elva turned a few pages and continued to read to an absolutely quiet audience:

> My whole childhood, I never had a bed.

My mind raced. When I had read this myself several hours earlier, I had thought, "Neither did I." Now I knew I had misread. I had read, "My whole childhood, I never had a bed to myself." Elva had never had a bed.

She continued:

In the one-bedroom rancho where I was born, my apá suspended a wooden box from the exposed rafter in the ceiling. My amá made a blanket nest for me in the box. It hung free in the air over my parents' bed, within reach of both. If I cried, they would swing the box.

We heard pieces of Elva's story, a story she told to an audience of non-Mexican Americans. She left her successful career of wool crepe suits to share her tale for several reasons. Many of us in the audience thought about the stories we silence when we bring Mexican Americans into the corporate world, which includes the world of education.

On other occasions Elva read portions of her book in southern Texas and many migrants and former migrants heard their stories in hers. Maybe her decision to tell her story will lead them to share theirs. Maybe silence will become voices.

As teachers we decide if the work in our classrooms honors our students' selves or forces them to live underground, as Elva did in order to succeed. In her story, from first grade through a master's degree from Stanford, she learned to hide her self in order to do well. Elva focused on math and science, where right answers reign. In reading and writing, where subjectivity enters teachers' evaluations, she knew her Mexican Americanness interfered with teachers' views of her potential.

Elva found her self when she was in her forties. In the process of writing, she discovered that her beautiful memories of growing up as the youngest child in a family of six were not always wonderful. Writing uncovered layers of meaning she didn't realize existed. As Elva's story became complex, she gained a deeper appreciation for her self, and as she shared her stories with her siblings, they all grew closer. When Elva realized the power of writing, she decided to write more, and is now working on her second book.

Elva's story symbolizes what I've learned about reading and writing. When we studied the students in Manchester, we found triple spin-offs from effective evaluation. The student-evaluators found value in (1) themselves, (2) others, and (3) their work.

When this is what an evaluation system fosters, the strong voices of readers and writers emerge.

Decisions

People who read and write frequently and regularly make lots of decisions. At a minimum, they need to decide what to read and write. They don't write or read only when given an assignment. Someone who waits to write until told what to do isn't an independent reader and writer. This person needs to step into the uncertain territory of real readers and writers in order to become one.

The hardest and easiest part of writing is knowing what to write about. It is what students need to practice most. Once they live amidst writers and readers in a daily workshop for a couple of months, they realize the abundance of writing possibilities all around them. Then the problem becomes "What do I write today?" The writer has more ideas than she can write about. A writer never finishes!

The same holds true for readers. Nonreaders often can't find something to read; they just can't find anything that looks interesting or possible. However, after they've lived for a couple of months in a classroom in which they are members of a daily readers-writers workshop, a new problem starts to emerge: "What do I read today?" Too many newspapers, books, and magazines amass themselves on the desks of readers, beside their chairs, and on the floor nearby. Readers wonder how many different things they can be in the midst of reading at one time.

Students are often in the midst of three choices: one easy, one hard, and one medium. Teachers of young children respect their desire and need to reread their favorites over and over. These children retain the hallmark behaviors of toddlers who insist that someone read the same book repeatedly. Their teachers read some books repeatedly to the class, appreciating the children's need to gradually understand the mysteries of a book. As children listen to favorites, and reread them, they become fluent. They feel the rhythm of readers. They excitedly say, "I can read this! Listen!" These books become easy.

The expectation to read easy books relieves tension in many elementary classrooms. Weak readers don't have to hide their books or feel uncomfortable. All students read easy books. When asked "What are you reading?" any student in the class may answer with the title of a book that is easy, medium, or hard.

The importance of reading hard books—or other difficult printed material—sometimes escapes us. Young children sometimes use hard books as markers. By trying to read parts of one book off and on for weeks or months, until they can finally read it all the way through, they know they are getting better. At other times, encouragement to spend time with hard books allows students to study photos and captions in information books in which the majority of the text is too difficult to read.

Hard books belong in the diet of adults and older students, as well. Sometimes a book is difficult because it just isn't interesting, but it's required for a course, or we need parts of it for a paper, or it's on a topic of interest to a friend and we want to read just enough to know what the friend is into.

Sometimes a requirement to always keep an easy, a medium, and a hard book going allows older students to save face. Those who aren't strong readers can be seen with hard books and no one will suggest they put them away.

Upon occasion, students who know they are weak readers choose books they know are a bit too hard and with unbelievable drive they pursue them, reading every word. To not have to restrict one's self to simple books can be some students' way out of the poor-reader box they find themselves in.

Medium books, or "just right" books, or books at their instructional level are the books young children choose, saying, "This is the book I've chosen to learn to read." Every new or beginning reader has a book or other printed material about which she can say, "This is the book I'm workin' on," which is very different from simply, "This is the book I've chosen." These students do not spend all of their time just going through books. No, they purposely conquer page after page, day after day, until they can read a book flawlessly. When they feel the rhythm and music in words, they know they can read.

I vividly recall a second-grade girl in Stratham who wanted to read to her class in the school library. I was a researcher in the library and this sounded fine to me, so Louisa chose a book and tried to read it to me. It was a book with only one sentence per page, but it was about a trip to the dentist and some of the words of the world of dentists' offices are tough. I helped Louisa in her classroom when she read it the first time and said I'd be back in a few days, after she'd had time to practice.

I returned, and she could read it only a bit better. Louisa had hardly practiced and I learned we were in a situation new to this child. No one had ever before placed her in a position of choosing a book to learn to read. Throughout Louisa's short career as a reader she had never read for perfection. She always went on to something else before she had completely learned to read anything. I, however, expected perfection on the part of students who read to their class in the library. Reading with an audience in mind is as important as writing for one. Louisa started to get the notion of practice. After a few days I invited her into the library to read to me again. She had trouble with only one word and promised to practice that page.

I said she could read to her class the next day. As she sat on the child-sized chair and read to her classmates scattered on the carpet before her, I sensed something but didn't know what was going on. This usually squirmy bunch of children sat unbelievably still. When Louisa finished her perfect rendition of this book, they clapped! This was not our custom in the library, and I remained confused. Later, her teacher explained. This child had, within that very occasion, gained recognition among her classmates as a reader. This applause welcomed her in. Until this day, no one had heard her read fluently. As she read, they all, in effect, held their breaths for her to succeed, and she did. Louisa took a humungous step and now could take off.

Reading "just right" books is what older students and adults do for the majority of their time as readers. We want a book that is just right in terms of what we enjoy. No matter how strong someone's recommendation is, I often know what I will like and strike off on my own path. Right now I'm reading mostly books by women of color with main characters who are also females of color, but yesterday I bought three books, and only one fits my self-imposed criterion: *Soul to Soul* by Yelena Khanga (1992).

I also bought *Cold Mountain* by Charles Frazier (1997). Because I'm a new resident of Virginia, everyone asks if I've read this book, set in the South. I also bought *Harry Potter and the Sorcerer's Stone*, by female author J. K. Rowling (1998). The *Harry Potter* books are the hottest new titles and I want to read at least one. Two of these three purchases, I predict, are just right, and the third one should be easy for me, because J. K. Rowling writes for upper-elementary readers, even though adults account for many of her sales.

In classrooms in which students always have at least one book of their choice going, and in which they frequently and regularly share them, they know who they are as readers. They evaluate themselves all the time. Wise book choices require them to do so.

All of the above also relates to writing. Writers have more than one task going. They write easy thank-you notes, hard speeches to deliver at school board meetings, and medium mealworm observations for science. They purposefully choose to try forms of writing that will stretch them, intentionally try strategies others have shared, and consciously use skills with increased care.

All of this writing and reading sets up huge diversity in a classroom. Rich readers-writers workshops honor and challenge the learners' decisions and don't pit one person against another. With so many kinds of reading and writing going on, competition flies out the window. There is room for lots of learners, all different.

Time

It takes time for students to become evaluators of themselves—to learn reflective thinking habits and to use them. Everything takes time. Time for evaluation, time for instruction, time for writing, time for reading. Time for the students to grow into their identities as writers and readers.

Writing instruction brings about huge changes in how our students and we spend our time. When I learned about the importance of workshops, I realized I could no longer conduct a predominantly lecture-based class at the University of New Hampshire. The teachers in my classes can't spend the majority of their time listening to me profess about what teachers do when they teach during workshops. I believe in workshops and create them in my classrooms.

This was a significant change for me and for most of the teachers in my classes. I set aside time for them to write and read during our university class sessions and time to talk about their writing and reading, the forms writers use, and what they might write and read next. When I manage to set up these writing workshops effectively, my students become engaged in their work and start to call themselves writers and readers. This, however, is not easy, even with years of practice on my part. Many teachers do not come to a university class intent on changing their identity from nonwriter to writer or nonreader to reader. Neither do their students.

It is no less complicated to turn around a class of sixth graders. If their former teachers didn't create effective workshops in which these students viewed themselves as writers, it probably won't occur that this will happen to them in sixth grade. They don't walk into sixth grade thinking, "I'm going to change my identity from nonwriter to writer."

So, the challenge begins. A person can only say, "I'm a writer," if she writes. And, she can't become a better writer if she isn't a writer in the first place.

The same goes for readers. Too many sixth graders enter their classrooms saying, "I've never read a book." Never! Some are weak readers but aren't the least bit interested in becoming better at something they have little interest in doing in the first place. Many of those who don't read know how, but the intrigue of reading has yet to pull them in. Similarly, teachers enter my classes saying, "I don't read. I don't have time."

The challenge continues. I not only want the teachers in my classes to be writers and readers, I want them, and myself, to continually evaluate ourselves as writers and readers. This is impossible, I've learned, until partway into the course. We must do a considerable amount of writing and reading before we can say, "This is what I do well as a writer," or, "This is something new I've just learned to do as a writer," or, "This is what I want to learn to do to become a better reader."

But the story is different for first graders. They come ready to go! They are in school to learn to read. Little children begin with confidence, and Monica Jones, a first-grade teacher who is a student in my class, bends over backward to avoid shattering it. She treats her little children like crystal and repeats to herself a hundred times a day, "These little children are readers. It's my task to find out what they can do and help them do more." Some of her children can tell a story to go with pictures, some can talk about books, and two can read simple books. They read to others and this reading thing spreads as fast as this teacher can engineer it.

These little children are also writers, and they know it. When Monica approaches them with crayons and an assortment of paper and asks, "Can you write?" the vast majority say, "Yes!" and reach for her treasures. They create pictures of events, drawings of individual objects, and lists of words. A handful write messages and stories. Monica exudes as much excitement for their work as they do, and she tells them specifically what she is excited about, "This purple flower is my favorite."

"Me too!!"

The juggling act Monica negotiates as their teacher often challenges her. In order to evaluate herself as a teacher, she, the other teachers in my class, and I talk about what is going well, and what is not. This takes courage, but until I know what each of my students wants to do in order to become a better teacher of writing and reading, I cannot effectively help them.

I assume that the teachers who enroll in my classes do so because they want to change as teachers. I require them to identify, write, and talk about something in their teaching that works and something that bothers them. Before they can do this, they read professional articles and books, discuss these with classmates, and become acquainted with various possibilities within the teaching of reading-writing. About one-third of the way into the semester, the teachers announce to the class their specific strengths and weaknesses. They evaluate themselves; they move forward with intent.

Some of them experiment with poetry instruction, others create new formats for book groups, and some want to learn how to incorporate writing into math. Their goals vary tremendously. Once I know what they want to learn, I help them design experiences that will give them the practice they need to learn the new teaching processes they want to explore. They try out their new ideas in their own classrooms or, if they're not teaching yet, in the classrooms of friends.

Reaching all of them is not easy for me. This kind of teaching stretches me, and I constantly work on my own teaching skills. I evaluate myself along with my students. They all know what I consider my strengths and what I am working on within a particular semester to improve my own teaching processes. We are in this together.

Learning to teach is a lifelong, never-ending task, as is learning to write and read. The teachers in my classes immerse themselves in their goals and then stop, step back, and say, "This is what I do well, and this is what I'd still like to learn."

There is no way to shortcut this process. It takes a lifetime to learn how to skillfully organize classrooms of readers and writers.

Response, Response-ability, Responsibility

Sometimes for inservice sessions I conduct with teachers, if they are midyear, I ask each teacher to picture the one student of hers who needs the most support. They each write a list of everything their particular student knows and can do. Then, in groups of three, they talk about their students, telling the others only what this student can do and does know. As I walk around the room I do not hear a single, solitary negative thought expressed by any teacher about any student.

Next, each teacher writes nonstop for ten minutes in this chosen student's voice, a personal narrative about something he can do, something he knows, or something he feels positive about. Then, each teacher reads it aloud to her group for response. The others find out as much as they can about each student's strengths and potential. Again, as I walk around, I do not hear a single negative thought expressed by any "student" about herself.

This can be a transforming experience. Many of the teachers start to evaluate these students in terms of what they *can* do rather than otherwise, and some basic tenets of response enter our discussion of this exercise. We realize that we can manipulate our perceptions of others. We can train ourselves to see the positive, and this influences our ability to respond to these students in the supportive ways they desperately need.

These students, in turn, eventually see themselves as learners, persons who know something and have the nerve to try learning something new. Only from a firm foundation can these students take the huge step into the unknown that they must take if they are going to declare, "My goal is to read a chapter book. I've never read one." Any step into new territory brings with it the possibility of failure, and these students have experienced more than their share of failure. They test our ability to provide huge quantities of supportive response.

Response serves as a booster seat for readers and writers. It allows them to reach further and it provides an incredible influence. Our response to others and to ourselves is so real. We become what we think. We are what we think about all day long. What goes through our minds as we walk around a classroom? How do we choose to look at our students?

We train ourselves to see what counts, what will help each student to see his potential. Optimism reigns. We take attitude lessons from the person who, when he finds one lone sock in his dryer, thinks he has an extra!

Of two basic ways to look at the world, evaluators of readers and writers work incredibly hard to become supportive responders. We strive to erase our profession's red-pen heritage. Instead, we search for value in what our students see and do as readers and writers.

Similarly, we create a system in which students share and seek value in one another. They know a great deal about their classmates and know whom to approach when they need content or information about skills and strategies. When response creates a classroom of learners who purposefully move forward, an effective response system hums.

Self-Discipline

On Sunday, August 22, 1999, in *The Daily Progress* newspaper of Charlottesville, Virginia, I read an article titled "The Write Couple," by David Maurer. About George and Susan Garrett, two local writers, the account began:

> After writing more than 25 books, a passel of short stories, poetry and three feature films, George Garrett knows one thing for sure. At times it can be oh so hard keeping one's backside placed firmly on the writing chair. There's a myriad of distractions that can conspire to move one's attention from the written work to wandering ways.
>
> With hat in hand, Garrett has often tried to slip out the front door of his home and distance himself from his writing tasks. But in order to make his escape, he has to pass his wife's writing room.
>
> Many times the husband will find his wife diligently typing away on her computer keyboard. Humbled, Garrett will often slink back up the stairs to his retreat, plant himself down before his ink-stained desk pad and re-establish a communication link with his Muse.
>
> "I think if Susan was doing something other than writing, I would find more excuses to goof off," Garret said. "I'm conscious of her discipline and it forces me to get back to mine."

We structure our classrooms with regular, frequent workshops in which everyone writes, reads, evaluates, and responds. These work sessions enable students to become so engaged they develop the discipline they need to keep themselves on task.

The structure the teacher provides when she sets aside predictable times for all the aspects of writing and reading allows the students to plan ahead. They know when they will write and read again, when they will share, and that they will receive helpful response. The system supports them, sweeps them in, and they want to remain a part of things. They start to amass some work.

During our research in Manchester, a chant evolved among the researchers to describe a succession of student behaviors that shows the process self-disciplined learners use: *"Collect, select, reflect, project,* and *affect"* (Hansen 1998b). First, *collect.* Readers collect titles of books and other materials they have learned to read or have read. Writers collect pieces of writing they have drafted, and, in some cases, brought to final copy.

With these collections, learners can start to see themselves as readers and writers and can *select* samples that best show who they are as readers and writers. These evaluators place this evidence of who they are in portfolios or in some other safe place. This is their proof to themselves and others of what they have tried.

These learners then *reflect* upon their selected work. They accompany all examples of their writing and evidence of their reading with explanations of why they decided to place those items in their portfolios. A child may have three book titles in her portfolio, and when we read her self-evaluation, we learn that they represent a newfound interest of hers in hot air balloons, or maybe the three are her first three chapter books, or maybe they are three books her fifth-grade tutor helped her learn to read. The child's reflection requires her to create a statement in which she tells herself and others what she has pursued.

To *project* into the future is next. The student looks ahead to what he will do with his time. He thinks about what he wants to learn as a reader and writer, discusses his options with others, and makes a decision about what to do next. The ability to set reasonable goals is a vital skill for a learner to acquire (Hansen 1996a).

Last, *affect*. The process of determining what one's self will do next assures some control and affects a person's life. The person is less likely to be scattered, to bow to the beck and call of various other persons and situations. This person can create a focus and gain a sense of purpose within the swirl of a day's busyness. This awareness of being able to affect one's own life helps a learner gain a feel for what the notion of self-discipline is all about.

Hmmmm . . .

Sometimes I wonder about all this *self-discipline*. Even though my own experiences with myself, friends, and students of all ages led me to realize the importance of being goal-directed, I wonder if all successful learners move forward with a conscious purpose. Maybe some of us become better writers simply by writing in a journal every day with no intent to become better, only a determination to wrestle with our thoughts. Maybe some of us learned to read in an almost magical way while nestled under Father's arm on the couch or when swept into the hum of a well-loved teacher's classroom.

I think I see self-discipline enter a young reader's life as the various elements of evaluation all come into play. He hears about Monica's own goals for herself as a reader and he knows he will change throughout his life. His *response* to her when she shares a biography leads him to a new section of their school library and a new world of fascinating persons. He decides to write mini-biographies of his classmates, a challenge that directs him for weeks.

The *time* students devote to their work and reflections upon it allows them to feel the possibilities in their future and realize the many *decisions* they can make about it. They can accomplish a great deal and travel circuitous routes into interesting tangential terrain along the way. They don't have to be so driven by a goal that they can't all of a sudden work with two friends to create a class newspaper.

The various *voices* in a busy classroom tug upon and support the writers and readers as they talk about what counts, what matters, and where they fit into all of this. The goals they set are influenced by the particular people in the class and groups they work in. In the most recent evaluation course I taught, one quiet primary teacher had been an art teacher in a former life, and several others in this class of twenty teachers sought to bring her voice into the center of things. They used her as a resource for their work, and not only did she teach some of them how to use watercolors, but their interest in her gave her the courage to experiment with a digital camera, transforming her work as a photographer.

E-value-ation, when felt as the response-ability of finding value in others, can turn a classroom into a setting in which readers and writers create work they value.

Voices | Three

Learning is the very essence of humility, learning from everything and from everybody. There is no hierarchy in learning. Authority denies learning and a follower will never learn.
—*Krishnamurti*

Isn't that a fascinating quote? At first I thought, "A follower will never learn?" Yes, a true follower never questions; he just mutters, "Yes, teacher." No voice.

Silence disturbs us at this time when our country strives to overcome decades of injustice within our schools. Jennie DeGroat (1997), an educator who is a member of the Navajo Nation, writes about programs for Navajo children and families that fail to honor their culture. "People are always trying to change us to make us better. Better at what? That's all I have to say" (114). Jennie speaks bravely for her people and for their voices, which have been silenced by authorities who don't value them. Having others listen to their words can change the Navajo. They know they can make a difference.

Their situation, in unexpected ways, finds a counterpart in classrooms of suburban America. When a teacher from one of our New Hampshire research projects moved to another state to teach in an affluent system, she found that her third graders had spent their first two years of school in classrooms in which silence was golden. She said, "It's new to them to share, to have people who want to listen to them." Her writers now hear their spoken and written voices. Each child has her own sound, her own voice, her own thoughts to be honored.

When Lois Lowry wrote *The Giver* (1993), she received hundreds of letters from readers who resolved her ending in many different ways. What a delight! All these opinions! She wanted her readers to find their own resolutions, and they did. There isn't a right one.

As a writer, I've learned that it's impossible to lead a group of teachers to agreement about my own book *When Learners Evaluate* (1998b). The teachers in all of my classes are at different places in their careers and in what they do when they evaluate and teach reading-writing. From my book, they take what works for them and their students. Twenty-five teachers who read my book, with me as the professor, do not become clones.

So, I've learned to ask, "What does this chapter mean to you?" The many responses fascinate me. We all become enriched as we hear the various insights in one set of ten pages. Then I tell them what it means to me, and they sit, eyes bright, amazed, and say, "Really?"

"No," I say, "but that's what it means to me today."

Diverse Voices Work Together

Vinnie was a compulsive second-grade writer in Manchester. He was the only one in his class with a yellow number 2 pencil stuck behind his ear and the only one who wrote messages on the margins of all his papers. He could also talk circles around many children and adults. One day he told researcher Jane Kearns about the draft he and his friend James had started seventeen days earlier, "on five and today it is twenty-two. That's a long time."

During share time Vinnie raised his hand to share, but someone called on James. Thin, frail, even fragile, James toed the masking tape mark on the floor and began to read from his and Vinnie's collaborative draft. Shy, his voice didn't carry and the students asked him to read louder. He fell back into the teacher for support and started over. When he finished and the students raised their hands to respond, James called on Vinnie.

Vinnie rose with a sheet of paper rolled into a thin cone, and said, "Here's something I just invented. It's a microphone. See. Lift this and you can talk. Then press it to turn it off. You can use it when you share next time."

James was Vinnie's special friend and James needed help. Vinnie stepped in. The two boys often wrote together, and their writing supported their friendship, as happens in many classrooms (Phinney 1998). The two boys were as different as night and day, and they worked together in this classroom where the teacher had taught them that every voice counts.

One summer, on the first day of my New Hampshire Writing Program (NHWP) class, *Evaluation in Literacy*, the teachers challenged me. The twenty teachers taught grades 1–12, regular and special education, across the United States and Canada, with experience ranging from zero to more than twenty years. Terrific diversity. However, they didn't all see it that way. Many of them had attended the NHWP in previous summers to take the

Teaching of Writing and/or the *Teaching of Reading and Writing* courses, in which the students met for two-thirds of each day in heterogeneous groups to work on their own literacy and for one-third of each day in homogeneous groups, by grade level, to learn about pedagogy.

They expected to do the same this summer, but heard otherwise when I explained our daily schedule: "We will all be together all the time. We won't separate our own literacy from our study of pedagogy, and we won't separate ourselves by grade level."

"Why not?"

"I'm teaching this course on *evaluation in literacy* because I'm involved in research on evaluation in an elementary-secondary project in which the teachers of all grade levels, subject areas, regular and special education meet biweekly to talk about examples of students' evaluations of themselves. We listen to what students say about their work and about the classroom situations that surround them. We see the insides of each other's classrooms, whether we teach high school family and consumer studies courses or first grade. We get many ideas from each other.

"The middle school English teacher borrows a teaching process the elementary special education teacher just created. It works! The diversity in the group gives us many more ideas than if we were all special education teachers or middle school English teachers."

Similarly to Dyson (1997), I learned about the powerful force of evaluation in a mixed group where difference was seen as a possibility, not a problem, and I have structured my summer school class accordingly. I requested my new class of diverse teachers to go along with me. I asked them to follow, and they did so grudgingly. I believed diversity would prove worthwhile to them, and I hoped they would come to value and learn from the range of voices in our class. They gradually did.

One day a fifth-grade teacher in the class wrote about the comments she had received from parents the previous spring when her students had shared their portfolios for a portfolio night. She reads her paper to our class and we heard one parent say, "A portfolio is a complete review of my daughter's progress and gives me a better understanding of her learning than A/B grades." Another said, "Thank you for providing us with this wonderful opportunity to spend one-on-one time with our son."

As our class discussed her paper, a high school teacher said, "I just read *Standards for the English Language Arts* [1996]. The issue of ownership and responsibility is in there, and your children certainly experienced it." Yes, others said. The fifth graders had talked about their work with an understanding of what it was for and what they had learned. They hadn't just routinely gone through the process of completing assignments.

JoLeigh Kirkland, one of the other high school teachers, said, "I'd like to move toward that." JoLeigh knew that would be difficult, given the many students she always has, but, in the fall, she began to give her urban students increased responsibility. Instead of telling them what to write about, she helped them find something they valued in their own lives to write about. At first they fussed—royally. Gradually, as they shared their writing, they became aware of aspects of themselves to explore via writing, and more and more of them became involved (Kirkland 1997). Finally, the majority came to like this new way of doing English, through which each of their very different voices was heard in all its glory.

By the end of week two, my summer students felt the combined energy of their various voices. They had learned to hear value in one another's experiences and goals. Their enthusiasm swept them into a new project. Hope Jenkins, a fifth-grade teacher from New Jersey, suggested that the class write a proposal to create an issue of *Primary Voices K–6*, a publication of the National Council of Teachers of English (NCTE). Right away, we had to deal with a conflict. This is a journal for elementary teachers, and we were not a group of such. We decided to propose articles by secondary teachers, as well, to show our newfound belief in diversity. NCTE accepted our proposal and we began work on what became the October 1997 issue.

As we neared the end of our summer course, one of the high school teachers commented, "The philosophy of this class has hit me. I've considered changing my teaching for years, but now I will." Her words struck me as odd. She had been in the summer program at least twice before and she was just now thinking seriously about change? The philosophy of our course was no different than that of any in the summer program. But, maybe it was. We, in our study of evaluation, purposely challenged and studied our values. Given the importance of diversity in today's schools, we addressed it, and discovered that the worth we saw in one another brought fundamental changes into our lives the next fall.

One secondary teacher returned to her district and gave in-service presentations to elementary teachers. These workshops gave her opportunities to continue to be among elementary teachers and to continue to learn from this new source of information recently made real to her. Viewing people who are different from us as persons in whom we see value is a mission of our literate classrooms (Bauer 1999). Bringing everyone's voice into the chorus takes much planning.

Individual Voices Gain Strength

In *Through My Eyes*, Ruby Bridges (1999) wrote about her lonely struggle in 1960 as the only black child in one newly integrated school in New Orleans. She spent most of the year alone with her first-grade teacher, while a handful of other first graders, all white, spent several months in a classroom down the hall. Ruby integrated the school. Only toward the end of the year did the community integrate her classroom.

Ruby's little voice made a huge difference, but she didn't realize it until she was about forty years old and started to hear her voice in documentaries and see her little self in old news clips. "I began to feel that my life should have a greater purpose. . . . That's what led me to establish The Ruby Bridges Foundation. . . . I believe we must turn inner-city public schools into great schools. All of our schools should be good enough to attract a healthy racial mix, which I believe leads to the most effective learning for everybody" (57–58).

In our Manchester project we learned how difficult it can be to create classrooms where students hear the voices of others. When we started our research there, we invited students to use their portfolios to show their answers to this question: "Who am I as a reader-writer?" In too many cases, students said, "I'm not." In many cases they did reading-writing work in school, but they didn't label themselves readers or writers. So, their portfolios lay empty, and rightfully so.

The teachers and students tried to figure out how to rectify this situation. Some of the sixth-grade girls started to bring artifacts from home such as cards from relatives. They saw themselves as readers-writers in a bigger context than school. We researchers and teachers, of course, should have thought of that, but instead they did, and we jumped on it. Soon, via the biweekly meetings of the teachers and researchers, everyone started to talk about readers-writers through this broad lens, and more students put entries into their portfolios with accompanying explanations about their choices.

But, for some students, the task remained impossible. "Read or write on my own? You've got to be kidding." Little children innocently—as young children often do things—solved this dilemma. When we opened the portfolios to evidence of reading-writing from home, one of the first-grade girls understood this to simply mean something important from home and brought in a necklace. "My daddy gave this to me before he went to prison." Well, her little voice was heard, not only by her classmates, who knew more about people going to prison than I certainly did at their age, but by us, in a larger sense.

In our meetings we talked about the importance of artifacts to show who we are, to help us identify ourselves, and to help others get to know us. For some students, it is easy to simply write and read their writing to the class, and in that way, others hear their voices and grant them a space. But for others, bringing in an object opens the door. With the recognition their classmates afford around the Author's Chair (Graves & Hansen 1984), an object allows some students to place themselves on this seat of vulnerability.

We learned about one sixth-grade girl's gradual disillusionment with tae kwon do, one first-grade boy's difficulties as he and his father lived in their truck, and one fifth-grade girl's challenge to care for her handicapped brother. Each student needed to be heard, and for some who hadn't been heard for years, their coming-out reminded me of a butterfly carefully testing its damp wings. But, fly it must. Similarly, the children's voices must be heard.

As we listened to the individual children who had found our format unworkable, we changed. Using students' evaluations as our guideline when we revised the reading-writing program made the difference. When they knew we heard them, some children planned occasions when their voices would be heard by all. Carmelita created her identity in book discussions. When she brought a spider as part of her response to *Spider Boy*, by Ralph Fletcher (1998), the students noticed and heard her.

Diane Parker (1997) wrote about drama as a way to strengthen readers' voices. She told the remarkable story of Jamie, a child she taught in grades K–2, who became a writer, reader, and "confident leader." Among other aspects of their literate classroom, Jamie and her classmates talked about and performed their own interpretations of children's literature. As they valued one another's thoughts, the young students gained confidence in their own voices.

Gaining Strength Through Trust Patricia McLure's (Newkirk & McLure 1996) first- and second-grade children tell stories when they share various children's literature books in small groups. A Christmas book leads to stories about Tic Tacs, stitches, and weddings. Pat, rather than use her adult criteria to determine what it means to keep a discussion on task, asks the children at various segues, "What made you remember that right now?" The children always know how one story leads to another. When the rules for talk are the children's rules, the children feel comfortable. Even the quiet children speak in these groups.

In order for her children to feel comfortable in all-class discussions, Pat carefully teaches them how to engage in discussions so their tentative voices resound with the energy she hears in the small groups. Pat devotes the first two months of school to weaving the safety net her first and second graders need in order to let their little voices ring. The procedure begins when one child has as his classroom job to walk around, during writing-reading time, with a clipboard on which is a class list. He finds students whose names have yet to be checked for this round and who want to share at the Author's Chair that day. He makes a list of who will be first, second, and third.

At 9:15 the students rise, put away their work folders, and move toward the carpet. Pat doesn't say a word. The children know what to do when the clock face shows 9:15. Child number one sits on the little chair, the children cluster in front of the reader on a large piece of carpet, Pat sits at the back of the cluster with her clipboard ready to record the children's responses, and the reader waits. When the class is quiet, the child reads. When finished, the child says, "Comments, questions, reminders, remembers?"

Pat has taught them to tell the writer-reader what they noticed in the piece of writing, and they start to respond without a word from her.

"I noticed you put seeds in the apple you drew."

"Thank you."

"I like your tall grass."

"I know, it was higher past my head!"

The children often ask questions, such as, "What orchard did you go to?"

"I don't know."

"Was it the one over by the apartments?"

"I think so."

"That's Wellington's."

"Oh. Any more questions?"

"How many apples did you pick?"

The class continues to gather information and some tell their own stories as they express their genuine interest in the author-reader on the chair.

When the response wanes, the child says, "Thank you," and child number two takes her place.

During the first two months of school, Pat teaches the children possibilities for their comments, questions, and stories and gradually weans herself from the picture. By the end of October her voice is not heard at all during the entire process of three children sharing their writing, lives, or reading. The children know they can do this alone, by themselves, without help. This is very important.

Strong voices thrive amidst trust. These children know their teacher trusts them, and their teacher knows she can trust them because she has very carefully taught them what kinds of responses will encourage them as learners. She wants them to become readers and writers who care for one another.

When they feel the energy and support of the group around them, Pat starts to challenge them. She teaches them new writing techniques so they consider these aspects of writing when they compose. Some of them move toward length and start to write two-page compositions instead of one-page ones. Others stay with short compositions and learn to put spaces between words. Others learn to see the nuances in their favorite topics, for example, their friends. They become able to write with more detail about their various antics.

Trust Takes Time   Teachers of older students teach these same behaviors and may need to spend much more time on them than primary teachers do, depending upon the history of their students. I remember the day I visited Tim Hillmer's middle school classroom. He had read a draft of his own writing to his students, and then a student read to the group. After each, the students made comments. Comments only. They repeated back to each writer some exact words they remembered. Tim's students did this for two months. Two months. Then he taught them other responses, but first, he and his students needed to be sure that it was safe to share in their room. They knew their individual voices would be honored.

It is hard to send your voice into the space of a classroom. Even the teachers in my graduate-level classes fear reading to the class. However, they need to do this in order to realize how response feels. At the same time, these writers respond to their classmates, a skill they teach their own students. It requires much practice, but we delight in the vast range of voices in our class.

Strong Voices Mend Rifts

But, sometimes things go wrong.

In Julie Pantano's (1999) grade 8 class, her students begin each period in the corner of the classroom on a swatch of carpet, a few of them snuggled into beanbag chairs. They sit close together to read by themselves and to read to the class. They share whatever they are reading or writing, listen to one another, and respond to the person who shares. Julie works extremely hard to teach them to see value in one another and, when they respond, to show their interest in what the sharer knows. She wants them to be keen to learn from one another.

They gradually realize the significance of Reena's nature poems; they had not heard her voice for years, and she had not heard her own. They gradually realize the significance of Yanfen's letters to the editor, and the newspaper eventually publishes one. They find the passages Marsha reads to them from vegetarian magazines fascinating, if not controversial.

They feel the difference between this class and their others. In this one, they move from the Share Corner to their desks, which they always need to arrange into clusters. Julie shares this room with another teacher, who always has her students rearrange the desks into rows, with each student separated from everyone else.

The different roles the students play in other teachers' classrooms sometimes make it difficult for them to truly live the life

Julie wants them to live in her classroom. She expects them to interact with one another while they work, to take stances at odds with one another and her, and to do so with grace and respect. Julie and her students have many heart-to-heart talks. She knows she expects a lot from them, and she knows she will not relent.

One day when a boy began to read from the Author's Chair, one of his buddies uttered an under-his-breath-but-loud-enough-for-all-to-hear comment. It was not a favorable one. The author froze. The session ended.

The next day, no one volunteered to share.

On the following day, the fear of ridicule continued to keep everyone away from the Author's Chair.

Then, Julie, a vibrant young woman who does not hide her love from her students, brought a bag of candy kisses to the class. She distributed a few to each student, with comments about her concern and hopes for their reconciliation. She invited them to redistribute their handfuls to others, as tokens of goodwill and forgiveness. Amidst uncomfortable snickering, laughter, and swapping, these eighth graders ate, talked about their difficulties, and moved forward. They knew they had something special going, and they wanted to keep their class alive. They mended their rifts.

Rifts of all kinds occur in classes of all ages when students invest energy in writing, reading, and their lives (Gallas 1998). It's easy to cross over the moveable, invisible line between helpfulness and intrusion. I find I must apologize in my university classes when I offer too much advice to a teacher who only wants a hint of a suggestion. Truly listening, in order to know what the sharer wants, is difficult but possible.

When viewers see the videos from our Manchester project (Hansen & Staley 1996), the most common response is "The students work together so well." Yes, they do. However, maintaining this climate in which no voice feels silenced challenges everyone.

Hmmmm . . .

Mike was a first-grade student who found school rather stressful. In January he had only two items in his portfolio and they revealed his difficulties. He had a photocopy of a cover of a book and to accompany it, he had written his reason for putting this artifact in his portfolio: "I like this book. I read it every day. I'm almost a reader."

His other item was a scrap of paper on which he had crayoned *M I K E*. His written explanation of why he had this in his portfolio breaks the custom for the classroom. He hadn't written the typical self-evaluation statement the children usually composed. He had created this artifact with a dramatic purpose in mind, and his explanation took the form of a note to his teacher. Leave it to the little children to break our structures, jar our senses, and awaken our notions of what portfolios, artifacts, and self-evaluation statements are for.

This is what little Mike's note said: "Miss Ross, please call me Mike. I do not like Michael cuz kids make fun of me outside. Love, Mike."

Mike created these portfolio entries for an audience. He knew when, within the structure of his class, he could make his voice heard. His class met weekly for a portfolio share, when everyone who had added something new and who wanted to share could. Mike was ready.

He told his classmates, clustered around him, about the book, showed them the scrap on which he had written his name, and read them his note to his teacher.

A little girl named Kim started the class response: "I don't like to be called Kimberly." To the class, she added, "I like his name because he wants to be called that."

And everyone, including his teacher, called him Mike from that day forward.

Decisions | Four

The third graders in Jeanne Bennek's class in St. Paul, Minnesota, set goals for themselves as readers and work on them every day during their readers workshop. Gradually, their ability to set workable goals improves under Jeanne's guidance and, periodically, she asks them how this overall approach to reading class works for them. Of the various responses they express, their most prevalent comment is "I love all the time I have to read what I choose!"

In their short careers as writers-readers, these young children know what it's like to not have choice, and they value being able to make decisions. Teaching children how to wisely choose books is not necessarily easy, and Jeanne had the courage to give this new teaching venture a try, at least in part, because she welcomed a researcher into her classroom. Amy Smith, a former colleague of hers, who is now a researcher, wanted to know what these students and their teacher would do if their reading class were driven by the students' goals. Even though, to the children, the highlight of reading is to read books of their choice, the bigger decision about "What do I want to learn next in order to become a better reader?" now consumes much of their time and that of their teacher.

This decision can be very hard. It is difficult to teach readers what it means to generate options for goals, evaluate their comparative worth, and choose among them. Then, as these learners work, they need to continue to make decisions. Jeanne teaches them to regularly evaluate their needs in the midst of books, consider various resources, and choose those with the most promise as they purposely move forward by circuitous spurts and snail-paced sojourns.

Students' Decisions About Goals and Plans

When Jeanne's third-grade children set their own goals for reading and worked on them every day as the core of their reading class, they became readers in a way that Jeanne, who had taught for twenty years, had never before experienced. In their final evaluations of themselves as readers, many wrote about the plans they had for their summer reading. Prior to this year, Jeanne's students had never, on their own, set summer reading goals. Little Maggie was quite specific: "Now I have more faith in my reading because I know I can choose good books for myself. I can read chapter books. I can read anything!"

Jeanne's decision to embark on this goal-setting venture occurred midyear, when she and her children revisited the goals they had set at the beginning of the year. Her students had been doing this since kindergarten. Throughout her school, the children and teachers set one overall goal at the start of each year and revisit it at midyear to decide whether it needs to be changed. However, during the intervening months, the children never talk about their goals. If they accomplish them, it is by chance. The reading program isn't set up for the children to purposely work on their goals. Jeanne realized that this routinized goal-setting procedure did not impact her students' growth as readers, and this concerned her. She inched toward a decision (Meehan 1997/1998) to change her teaching.

Jeanne's worry about this system became something she could address when her friend Amy started to look for a classroom in which to collect her dissertation data. During her coursework, Amy learned about the importance of daily work by children on the goals they set for their own growth. She also realized that children often need to break their goals down into step-by-step plans in order for them to be workable. And, Amy had learned that the process of collecting their own evidence to document their learning process helps many students stay on task. In the classrooms she learned about (Hindley 1996; Carroll & Christenson 1995), the students regularly share their frustrations and delights with their teachers and classmates for support and help.

All of this sounded fine to Jeanne, but what she didn't know were the kinds of difficulties her students would have and what she would need to teach. This was all quite new to her. However, she stepped forward with confidence in her overall ability to teach, appreciated Amy's presence, and acknowledged her nervous excitement about how she would grow as a teacher of reading.

During the first few days, Jeanne and Amy learned about the wide range in the children's ability to set goals for their own growth, and these two women quickly learned new teaching roles as they helped the children create options for their goals. In general, the children set goals that either focused on a particular kind of information they wanted to study, on specific books they wanted to read, or on reading-writing strategies they wanted to employ.

Children Become Goal-Directed   Anna was a student who wasn't sure of herself. She had just written about avalanches and thought her writing was pretty good. When Amy met with her, Anna said, "Mrs. Bennek liked the details I used to describe the setting. I think it's interesting, too, because I saw a show about avalanches and then I put it in my writing. I want to learn more about avalanches." But, Anna wasn't sure if she wanted to write a reading goal about them. She decided to ask Jeanne for ideas.

When she did, Jeanne said, "So, let's make a list of possible goals."

On her Goal Sheet for her portfolio, Anna writes:

1. *Avalanches*

She stopped.

Jeanne wondered what else she was interested in, and Anna said she didn't know. Jeanne tried a different route: "What book have you been thinking you'd like to read?"

Anna sat, thought, and finally said, "The one you're reading to the class." She added it to her list:

2. *My Name Is María Isabel* [Ada 1995]

Jeanne led Anna down a third route: "What do you do well as a reader?"

Anna replied, "I know most of the words."

Jeanne said, "Yes, you do! I remember the other day when you read to your group from the Amelia Bedelia book. What do you want to be able to do to be a better reader?"

Anna replied, "I want to read with expression." She added it to her list:

3. *Read with expression*

Jeanne asked, "So, which of these three goals do you think you'll choose?"

Anna said, "The last one."

"Great, and what can your plan be?" Jeanne asked. "What are some things you can do to learn to read with expression? Why don't you think about this and talk to Ruana [Anna's friend] if you need ideas. I'll check back tomorrow."

Jeanne had to move on in order to confer with more children, but as she moved to another child's desk, she stopped for one second beside Ruana and said, "I think Anna may like to confer with you about her plans, OK?" Ruana smiled. Jeanne didn't know how far the two would get, but she thought Anna had chosen a reasonable goal. It was difficult for this hesitant child to read aloud with assurance and expression. Jeanne thought maybe she could video Anna someday when she read well. That could help send her on her way to becoming a more confident reader.

Jeanne conferred with Clare next. Clare's goal was to become an expert on dolphins. The previous year she had gone to Sea World, had seen dolphins, and had been "dolphin crazy" ever since. She wrote this plan to explicate her goal:

1. *I will read two books that I checked out of the library.*
2. *I will go to my dad's work and use his computer to go on the Internet to find out more about dolphins.*

Clare shed light on her goal and plan: "Dolphins have some toughness in life and some good things, just like me. Dolphins have to be careful of sharks, but they are good communicators. I have to be careful of my brother and I am a good communicator, too. . . . I will write a nonfiction piece about dolphins." Clare knew where she was going and how to get there.

Jeanne predicted her role as teacher would be to show interest and cheer Clare along her way. This turned out to be true. Clare didn't need much help. She had learned to challenge herself.

Meanwhile, Amy scanned the room and decided to go to Jake, who seemed at loose ends. His words confirmed her hunch: "I'm not really working on my goal. I don't really get it. . . . My mom helped me write this [the goal on his Goal Sheet in his portfolio]. She thought it would be good for me to read more books."

Later, Amy shared what Jake had said with Jeanne. For some time Jeanne had wondered how to bring a spark into Jake's interest in reading. She decided to start with the friends route. Jake and Matt played ball together, so maybe they could read together. Jeanne approached Jake with her idea in her head and said, "I'm wondering about your goal, Jake."

He showed Jeanne his Goal Sheet in his portfolio and said, "My mom thinks it would be good if I read more books."

"What do you think?"

"I guess so."

Jeanne introduced her option, but Jake worried that he didn't read well enough to read with Matt. They continued to generate possibilities, and Jake became excited about the possibility of reading every day with a first-grade buddy. Jeanne promised to check after school so, they hoped, Jake could begin the next day.

After two months with his new little buddy, Jake felt confident enough to read with Matt.

Matt, in the meantime, gradually learned about the process of setting a goal. When the class started this change in the reading program, he already saw himself as a reader and didn't understand the need for specificity in a goal. Matt's first goal was "to read more and more." However, he approached Amy one day and said he had made a big decision about his goal setting. He had evaluated his goal and decided he had to change it because he had written an impossible one. "I can never complete my goal because every time I read something I have to read more. . . . It will never end!"

With this realization, Matt created a new goal: to read all nine of the Matt Christopher books. "At least this goal has an end," he explained. His change exemplifies a common trend.

As children revise their goals, or write new ones after they have accomplished one, they tend to write more specific goals. Their evaluations of past work, their interactions with their classmates, and the skills Jeanne teaches all lead them to become better goal setters. Many of the children also write more immediate goals or weekly goals. They like finishing and sharing with one another.

Marie's sharing with the class may have influenced Matt's new, more specific goal. Her goal was to read a bigger book, *The Diary of Anne Frank*, and she was so proud when she finished it. She gave the class a stellar recap of the story, showed a certificate she made for herself to put in her portfolio, and led a discussion about the book. Then she asked, "Did anyone else accomplish something on their goal today?" Others shared. In general, the children get very excited as they talk about their goals. They are more aware of one another than they were before they started to share goals and they celebrate everyone's successes.

Some of them started to create *partner goals*, a term they came up with. Two girls set a goal to read to their younger siblings and set up a conference with the school librarian to ask her about interesting books to read to three- and four-year-olds. She suggested Bill Peet's books but the girls discovered that Bill Peet wasn't a good choice. The stories were too long. They told the librarian this! Everyone worked on the notion of creating workable goals.

Helping Students Help Themselves It's not easy for these children to create their own assignments, but to be able to do so is what it means to be an independent reader, and the children and Jeanne experience enough success to have the energy they need to work through the glitches. Jeanne sometimes intervenes when children's plans seem, to her, unwise or impractical. For example, one week Matt and Jake narrowed their choice of their next book to two titles, but couldn't find two copies of either book. So, they decided to read both, alternating between the two books every five minutes. Jeanne suggested they think of other options; in only five minutes they couldn't get into a story. They worked out a compromise and decided to alternate every other day for a week and then evaluate how it was working.

Whereas Jeanne oftentimes plays these instructive roles, she also plays another role. Jeanne loves to be a cheerleader. She is on the alert for children's accomplishments, large and small, and invites them to share those with the class. They see one another through eyes of respect and often get ideas for themselves.

Students' Decisions About Documenting Their Growth

What counts as evidence of a child's growth as a reader-writer? What matters? What does the student value as evidence? A real piece of writing shows more than a letter grade, and a book list shows more than a 76 percent score on a reading test. Real evidence shows what children actually can do, whereas letter grades or numbers only *represent* what a child can do. Four students could each receive a B, but they could be very different readers or writers. The full-size pages of portfolios or some other real documentation show more than the little boxes in grade books.

It was when our profession started to place importance on the processes writers use that many teachers started to collect samples to show students' growth. Collections of students' writing show their amazing changes, and parents, administrators, school boards, community members, teachers, and the students themselves all appreciate these displays. Not only do drafts show growth within a piece of writing, but, more importantly, an array of writing shows when a student tried something new and the ways in which a writer expanded.

However, without an explanation of what the pieces of writing or the book list shows, the onlooker may miss some important nuances of change. It is impossible to know the significance of a student's work to the child unless that student speaks for herself. Thus, we have learned to give students the responsibility of deciding what documentation to use, and what to say about it, in order to accurately tell their stories about themselves as writers who read.

When Amy Smith (2000) studied preschool children's changes as they learned to give reasons for the additions to their portfolios, she observed the following sequence:

1. Children gave "It's special," as their reason for making a choice.
2. Children included evidence of first-time creations, such as a photo of a block structure.

3. The youngsters began their reasons with "because." This represented a turning point in the children's thinking. When they started to see themselves as agents, their future reflections became more complex.

4. The students chose work that was not necessarily their best, but that they had worked hard to create. Erika chose a crayon rubbing "because it was tricky to do and I worked really hard on it" (207).

5. The children eventually chose artifacts they had created independently; one child said, "the teachers didn't write the words, I did" (207). Being able to create their own reasons is critically important in order for learners to realize their potential (Wilcox 1995).

When Carol Wilcox served as a researcher in Debbie MacLaughlin's second-grade classroom in the Beech Street School in Manchester, she worked hard to help the children see their growth and write about it in explanatory reflections. Carol loves the following story of the day Amanda wrote an effective reflection, and of how this knowledge spread among the other children.

One day in March Amanda shared her portfolio with Carol, who excitedly supported Amanda's accomplishments as a writer and then said, "You have lots in your portfolio that shows your growth as a writer, but you don't have as much about yourself as a reader."

Amanda only had to think for a second, "I can read chapter books now. My grammy gave me two chapter books for Halloween and I can read them now."

"Really, Amanda! Do you think you would like to show that in your portfolio?"

Amanda nodded enthusiastically. "I could bring the books and you could copy them. I'll bring them tomorrow."

The next day, she greeted Carol, chapter books in hand. They photocopied the cover of one, and Carol sat next to Amanda as she wrote her self-evaluation of her accomplishment. Carol had decided to sit nearby because she had started to worry about the children's sparse reflections. Carol thought if Amanda were left to her own devices, she would probably write, "This is a book I like," or, "This is a book I know how to read." What Amanda did write was:

I am putting this in my portfolio because it's funny.

Carol pushed, "That's why you want this in your portfolio, because it's funny? Is that the only reason?"

Amanda added to her reflection:

and it's the first chapter book I ever read.

Carol questioned more "Is it an easy book or a hard one?" Amanda wrote:

The words are easy. [see Figure 4-1]

Later that day, the class held a portfolio share, and Amanda shared her new addition. The children talked about her accomplishment, and Carol asked the class, "Which reflection will give a person who looks at Amanda's portfolio more information—one like Amanda read to you or one that only says, 'I am putting this in my portfolio because it's funny'?"

The second graders knew, of course, what answer Carol was looking for.

Their discussion continued, and Amy asked Amanda, "How did you know what to write?"

Amanda said, "I didn't, but Miss Wilcox helped me write this reflection."

Carol asked Amanda if she thought she could do it herself the next time.

Amanda looked a little dubious, but nodded her head yes. And, in fact, her new language patterns quickly rippled out into the class.

A couple of days later, Carol met with two small groups. In the first one, Dee shared her latest addition to her portfolio: two postcards she had received and had just read. She said, "I put these in my portfolio because they are from Miss Wilcox and I love what she wrote, and I love the pictures mostly."

Joe, remembering Carol's suggestion two days earlier, sensed Dee had also remembered. He thought she had "read" more words than she had written, and said so.

Carol quickly supported Dee, saying, "So, Dee, are you rehearsing a new reflection?"

Dee nodded, "It really says, 'This is a postcard from Miss Wilcox,' but I'm gonna get a new one of those [sticky notes] and I'm gonna write more." When Carol told Dee that she was writing better reflections, Dee responded, "I used to write one sentence, and now I'm writing more."

Figure 4-1. Self-evaluation.

Whereas length may not be everything, the children were starting to think in more detail about why they chose artifacts to show who they were as writers-readers.

In the second group Carol met with, Renee showed a cow picture she had drawn, which Carol had seen several times. The attached reflection said, "This is what I love." What Renee said, however, was, "I saw this little guy jumping in a corral of cows. I saw another cow at the fair, too." Carol asked her if she intended to write a new reflection, and Renee answered yes.

Heather then shared a tall tale she had written, with an attached reflection that read, "This is a tall tale." When Heather read it to the group, she added, "It's my best handwriting."

As Heather wrote this addition to her reflection, Val commented, "You're doing a very good job writing that reflection."

Heather responded by showing her new sticky note and saying, "See, it starts on the front and goes onto the back." These children were definitely starting to learn that their reflections were not to be just dashed-off comments, but self-evaluations of themselves that pointed out what they were learning to do.

Eric shared a picture he had created of himself and his dad on a Harley, accompanied by a reflection stating, "This is me and my dad on his Harley." Eric said, "I'm going to change it. My new reflection will say, 'My dad picks me up on his Harley during the summer, and he has a nice Harley and he has eight peggers,'" which, he explained, are those fancy handlebars that sort of curve up.

In his new reflection, Eric intended to elaborate on his original explanation by giving more information about his dad's machine and their visits. We gain additional insights into why his illustration is important enough to warrant a place in his portfolio. Oftentimes, the emotional content of an illustration, a piece of writing, or a book is what distinguishes its importance. Eric did not place this in his portfolio because it was the first time he drew a motorcycle; it verified his relationship with his dad.

When Eric and the other children in our research projects started to document their journeys, I initially expected them to show the various skills they had learned, but I soon learned that the emotions and content of what they were reading, writing, or drawing were often the driving forces. Children write and read to learn about their world from their earliest days. Who they are as writers and readers is much bigger than I thought when I pegged them as people who gradually acquire punctuation skills and comprehension strategies.

The little group with Eric, Heather, and Renee continued. It was now Val's turn and her new portfolio addition was a book she had written. Her reflection said, "This is my favorite book," but she said she was going to change it so it would read, "This is my favorite picture in this book. I made the book and it is my favorite."

Eric commented, "That reflection will be nice."

Val asked him, "Why do you think it sounds nice?"

" 'Cause."

Val became more insistent, " 'Cause why?"

Eric apparently had just quipped off his comment. He evidently didn't know why he thought it sounded nice, but he rescued himself by changing the subject. "Why are you going to change your reflection?"

"Heather's reflection gave me some new ideas."

The children were focused on this task of writing good reflections and, with the teaching of Carol and Debbie, they gradually improved. As they became more able to articulate their reasons for choosing specific artifacts, they started to think about what they were learning while midtask. Their decisions about their pieces of documentation helped them become increasingly aware of what they all could do as readers and writers.

Students' Decisions About Whom to Use as Resources

My first everlasting lesson about the importance of classmates to beginning readers occurred as I collected research data in Ellen Blackburn Karelitz's classroom (Karelitz 1993). Her students, none of whom had attended kindergarten, ranged from two children who could read to several who were quite inexperienced with books. Ellen didn't place them in reading groups, and we watched them during reading workshop.

The children chose books that other children in the class had already read. They often chose the books Ellen published. Starting on the very first day, she daily published one child's piece of writing as a hardcover book for the classroom library. When she had published one book per child, she started to publish their work less frequently, but the initial influx played a significant role in getting the classroom reading program off the ground.

The authors introduced their new books to the class, read them aloud, and led a discussion of them. They became quick favorites. These first books were often as short as three pages, and the children quickly learned to read them. During reading workshop the children often approached an author, book in hand, and asked, "Could you read this to me?" The writers swelled at this request; they loved to teach other children to read their books.

Children who read the literature of professional authors to the class received similar requests about books they had read.

What these young readers showed me was monumental. Those who could not yet read did not put themselves in a group with the other children who couldn't read. This, in 1981, was brand new to me. The only kinds of groups I had ever taught were homogeneous ones. However, when we studied the children, we learned the ever-elusive obvious. When a child can't read, that child goes to someone who can!

When we realized what the children were doing, Ellen encouraged this interaction. Now, many teachers do this. In order for their students to know who can read what, the teachers arrange for much sharing. Children not only read to the class but meet in small groups in which each child brings whatever book he is learning to read or has just learned to read. These groups change frequently in order for the children to become acquainted with as many different readers as possible.

In Patricia McLure's classroom of first and second graders, one of the class helpers goes around with a clipboard each Friday and children sign up for a day during the upcoming week when they would like to meet with a small group to share the books they are learning how to read and can now read.

Before too long, life for these beginning readers becomes more complicated. As more and more students learn to read books, more available choices sit on shelves. Students start to weigh an increasingly larger domain of factors when they decide what to read next. This new array of possibilities often becomes increasingly complicated over the years as readers become older, but sometimes it doesn't. As readers become more experienced, they often become more aware of who they are and can make quick decisions about what to reject or what to read.

Regardless of our age, we make many daily decisions about what to read, and large numbers of these are influenced by the other readers we know. Just as little children do not teach themselves to read, we typically do not survive as readers if we do not interact with other readers. The task of we who teach is to help all of our students realize which classmates can support their varying needs.

Classroom conversations often center around why people chose certain reading materials. Some students choose books because the students who can read them know how to teach others to do so. Helping others learn to read is a skill children need to learn, and teachers provide small-group and whole-class sessions in which they demonstrate what children might do when someone asks, "Will you read your book to me?" or, "Will you read this book with me?" or, "Will you listen to me try to read this book?" They learn to choral read, to read every other page, and to supply unknown words. They also learn to not supply words, to instead teach their friends to read ahead and return to try the unknown word when they have more context. They learn to see words as part of word families and to sound them out.

They study the strategies and skills they use and learn to teach them to others. This study of themselves as readers and writers helps solidify their own skills and helps them grow. Edward, for example, possessed computer expertise beyond many of his classmates. As two of his classmates watched with awe while he expertly manipulated the computer through a series of difficult steps, one of them quietly exclaimed, "Wow! How'd you ever learn to do that?" Edward, a child with sometimes shaky social skills, gradually refined his ability to serve as a resource for other writers.

Sometimes writers suggest specific books to each other because they think a book relates to a friend's current draft. One girl, for example, offered Dinah Johnson's *Sunday Week* (1999) to Demetria when she was writing about what she did on each day of her week. Demetria decided to write the names of the days in various colors, as a takeoff of the blue lettering used for the names of the days in Johnson's book.

Increasingly, writing and author studies are becoming an integral part of readers-writers workshops and students are much more knowledgeable about writers than they were several years ago. When I first started to study reading, many students could not talk about authors, much less their favorites. Now students can list not only writers they admire, but titles they enjoy and can tell me what differentiates one author from another. Often, when readers listen to classmates talk about various authors, their writing and reading decisions become influenced by what they hear, but sometimes the possibility of choosing books by certain authors needs to be pointed out.

In a classroom where a wide variety of materials exists, where the readers know one another and know what one another reads, they know who to go to when they want a good book of poetry, a worthwhile article about the uses of writing and reading in math, or information about wrestling. Readers and writers often look for materials because of specific content they are interested in. Some students choose sports magazines, the sports section of the local newspaper, and sports books. Others love books about dancers, artists, and bratty little sisters. The availability of a variety of reading materials is what enables some students to become readers.

In my graduate classes for teachers, I provide a variety of books and articles from which they choose. They focus their semester on the study of reading, writing, and/or evaluation in a way that appeals to them. They sometimes read the same books and articles as others in the class and appreciate comparing notes. At other times their conversations with classmates who haven't read a particular article or book add to their understanding of what they read. Sometimes they purposefully choose to talk with someone who has read a book or an article they haven't read because they think it might contain information they'll appreciate. Depending upon the other person's comments, they may read it.

Readers also base their decisions about what to read on how books make them feel and rethink their reason for being. They talk about ways a book connects to their lives differently than to anyone else's, what the author's approach to life seems to be, connections among various books, and what they see in books upon successive discussions of one title. To become readers, they live and relive the books and materials they read. Sometimes they choose to talk about books with certain friends, and at other times their teacher suggests difference: "Tomorrow we'll all talk about something we're reading or writing with persons we know less well than others." In this way, a reader's circle of persons to use as resources may expand.

Students often base their reading choices on what people with their same tastes read, and it takes time for a class of readers and writers to know one another well enough for this to happen. A considerable amount of sharing precedes smooth decisions about books. In Jan Roberts' third-grade class the children shared books for two months before the majority of the students were familiar with enough titles to be able to know of a title they wanted to read. Readers' tastes are very idiosyncratic and they need to find out what their own preferences are in order to become readers. Their personal likes and dislikes become apparent to them as they listen to, question, and observe the other readers in their workshop.

Choosing to Grow   When students become swept into the world of reading, they typically want to become better. They purposefully choose reading materials that will help them grow as readers. These students consider level of difficulty from various angles, and these possibilities often need to be taught to readers.

Often readers want an easy book; either they want to learn to read it or they already can and want to reread it. The sheer pleasure of reliving a book or of celebrating one's newly acquired reading expertise is a joy many students love, and they often choose to do so at a time when a special friend is available. This rereading can serve many purposes for readers of various ages. For young children it is extremely important as one way for them to solidify their ability to read.

Upon occasion, students thrive on challenge, but too much of a challenge becomes frustration. The amount of difficulty a student is willing to take on typically depends on the reader's specific purpose and who is available to help. Book buddy arrangements across grade levels often help less-experienced readers study materials or read only parts of books while searching for certain information.

Frequently students choose to read materials that are neither difficult nor easy, but their choice broadens their identity as a reader. One reader said, "I always thought newspapers looked boring, but lots of people read them, so I decided to read one—well, parts of one—every day for two weeks. They're not bad. It gave me something to talk about with my dad."

When some fourth graders in Manchester slipped into a lull in their writing, David pulled them out. At home one night, he watched his father become deeply engrossed in a book about Abraham Lincoln and the Civil War. David recognized his father's intense interest and decided he wanted to learn about Lincoln, too. The next day he checked out two books about Lincoln and, after diligent research, wrote a report. Other students found his report fabulous; David's great idea served as a seed. Presidential reports popped up on many desks, and David served as a ready resource.

The Benefits of Interaction   Overall, the benefits of interaction help many students. Pullout programs, however, can interfere with some students' opportunities to use one another as resources. When teachers realize this (Deshon 1997), they work to restructure their workshops so all children have time to benefit from the type of interaction with others they prefer, whether that be in class sessions or peer conferences. The ability to decide whom to use as a resource is a skill writers and readers hone; it's a lifelong process used by excited learners.

Hmmmm . . .

Jane Corbett's high school students reinforced my sense of the importance of interactions among readers. Some of them read their first entire book in her class. They had never been taught how to make decisions about books. They had been through all of their elementary and junior high years and had only read teacher choices, which some of them had never—yes, never—read.

Some of them had been in classrooms or schools in which a period of time was set aside regularly during which everyone read books of his or her choice, but a time to talk about these books was not set aside, and some students never did find something to read that interested them. Their reading program was not based on material they chose to read; their own reading was a sideline.

In Jane's class, they appreciate talking with one another and making their own decisions about what to read. They started to label themselves readers—for the first time in their lives.

TIME
To create the comfort zone
I know students need.
Many feel reserved, but
Each voice must be heard.

In order for her students to know one another well, Karen Boettcher's sixth graders redesign their classroom on the first day of each month. They rearrange their twenty-eight desks into any design they want, such as a jack-o'-lantern for October or a diamond for February (a heart would be too obvious!). Karen places only one restriction on them. At least one of the people they sit beside in their new configuration must be someone they have not yet sat beside. This monthly realignment enables her students to become better acquainted than they would if they sat beside the same persons all year.

Getting to know the various class members takes time but is necessary in order for them to feel comfortable enough to challenge themselves, to purposely step into unknown territory in order to try something new.

It Takes Time to Become Comfortable

For some students, an entire year doesn't provide the security they need. It took Anna, a primary child, two and half years to become comfortable. That's a long time. When she finally felt snug, learning to read became a possibility.

Anna was a young child I studied for three years when she was in the primary grades (Hansen 1989). As a girl who repeated first grade, she came to second grade with self-doubt. In December of that year I said to her, "You've been in second grade for three months. What have you learned about yourself as a reader?"

"I'm better," she said smiling.

"Show me what you mean, please," I requested, knowing she could. Anna had practiced more than one book until she could read each flawlessly.

"Listen," she said and proceeded to fluently read a book from her reading stack.

It had taken longer than we had expected for Anna to feel comfortable as a reader in second grade. The books she had learned to read in first grade were not in her second-grade classroom library. In September she swept her arm toward the collection and said, "Look at all those books. I can't read any of them." Anna ended up finding familiar books in the school library, and we learned of the importance of surrounding children with familiar literature at the beginning of each year. Amidst books they can read, the children reach toward more difficult ones. Without the security of books they know, some children feel lost in a sea of uncertainty.

It also took Anna a long time to feel comfortable because her close friends from first grade were not in her second-grade classroom. Many faces in most classrooms will, of necessity, be unfamiliar, and we learn to teach social skills so the children feel at ease with their new classmates. Mini-lessons on what to do when someone is alone at recess and on how to approach a classmate when you want that person to read to you can be very important.

Anna either had forgotten how to ask classmates for help with books or still felt uncomfortable asking these strangers for assistance, and she needed help from many people in order to learn to read. Anna had spent the summer with her family, an elderly uncle and aunt who loved her dearly but kept her in isolation. She spent months with these two adults and had not interacted with children. Until Anna made new friends, an extremely difficult task that took weeks, she couldn't become a better reader.

For a long time, the children practiced gentle ways to approach classmates at appropriate times and rehearsed their reciprocal roles as peer-teachers. Sometimes to simply stand by someone is the appropriate approach. When that student comes to a stopping point, she looks up, and the student who wants help asks, "Would this be a good time for you to help me?"

Sometimes when the person looks up, the child who wants help simply asks his question, "What's this word?" or "Can you come to the library with me?" or "Can I read this to you?" If the person can't help, she is obligated to assist with finding someone who can. In general, the person initially asked can help. The idea of the readers and writers workshop is to have in place a community of workers who are all aware of what one another is doing and who will offer or provide services when requested.

One way to help is to take time to slowly listen when someone reads. I became especially aware of the need to teach the

children to not jump in with their help on the day Anna read
City Mouse, Country Mouse to me. With the focus of our research
on self-evaluation, I could not step in when she read a word incorrectly and say, "Does that make sense?" I couldn't be the one
to evaluate whether the story line flowed. Anna needed to develop the habit of constantly thinking about the meaning.

As she read this particular book, she consistently reversed the
words *city* and *country*, but always kept right on reading. I wondered if she understood the story, and whether she would ever
correct herself. Finally, after several pages, she was confused
enough to turn to me and ask, "Which mouse in the picture is
the city mouse?" I clarified her confusion and Anna exclaimed,
"Oh no!" She promptly started the entire book over and reread it
correctly. Anna learned, through repeated experiences similar to
this, that it was her responsibility to monitor her reading, and
mine to respond when she requested help.

This also was the role she expected her classmates to play
when she read to them, and it is a role to teach in mini-lessons.
When a reader wants help from her partner she asks for it, and
that is when the partner provides it. Knowing the roles of the two
persons in a partnership enables children to feel comfortable.
They know what to expect.

We Support Students' Confidence Whereas it took a great deal
of time and effort for Anna to become a reader, she considered
herself a writer from the beginning of her years in first grade. "I
always know what to write about. I like to write. I'm hoping to
be an author." Our awareness of her evaluations of herself as a
writer helped us respond with this in mind, to preserve her sense
of herself as a writer. We felt her writing was often sparse, but
we were very careful not to shatter her confidence. She was growing and could show us exactly in what ways her writing was im-
proving. We took great pains to support her pace and direction as
she slowly moved from brief compositions such as "I love rain-
bows" to a Halloween story with dialogue among a ghost, a jack-
o'-lantern, and a cat.

Time alone did not create Anna's belief in herself as a writer.
The ways Anna, her teacher, and her classmates supported her for
months and years provided her comfort. In part from my study of
Anna, I now realize that when a student wants to read her writing aloud, it is up to that author to specify the kind of response
she wants. Anna only wanted me to tell her what I loved. That
was all. Then, she went to someone else to collect more love.

We Teach Social Skills Overall, as we learned from Anna about
her family, her friends, her writing, and her reading, we learned
about how much time it takes to weave a security blanket and to
teach the skills a child needs. Anna helped me realize the

importance of a very careful look at a child's academic and social comfort. Whereas our profession typically does look beyond the academic prowess of students, we often do not realize the necessity of social skills in order for students to be able to use classmates' expertise to learn. Without the ability to do so, the child can only rely on self and teacher; the former may be stuck and the latter may be busy.

Gradually, this little girl with many social and academic challenges became a part of the classroom. Specific efforts and time enabled her comfort zone to expand.

We Preserve Time to Write, Read, Talk, and Listen

Time to Write Julia Cameron (1998) wrote:

> What writers tell themselves while they procrastinate is that they just don't have ideas yet, and when they do, then they'll start writing. It actually works exactly backward. When we start to write, we prime the pump and the flow of ideas begins to move. It is the act of writing that calls ideas forward, not ideas that call forward writing. (87)

So true. This section of the chapter on time starts with writing. Someone who writes can call herself a writer; someone who doesn't set aside time, find time, allot time for writing, someone who doesn't write can't call herself a writer. This necessity for time became apparent in the early days of research on writing instruction, when two pieces of information collided.

1. People who call themselves writers, write frequently, usually daily.
2. Many teachers expect their students to write once a week, and this writing is typically not done in the classroom.

It's interesting how these pieces of information surfaced. When educators, the public, and students became frustrated with their inexpertness as writers, some researchers started to study the behaviors of professional writers, seeking direction. When asked, "How might people who are learning to write spend their time wisely?" writers' most common response was, "Write every day."

Other researchers observed in classrooms, surveyed teachers and students, and compiled data on the amount of writing students did—not much.

So, we learned. Writing is too hard to be learned with once-a-week practice. Teachers can provide their students with the best writing instruction in the world, but if students don't practice, they won't ever gain expertise.

Time to Read Many people read, and they don't write, and that's fine. In this section, however, I write about readers who are writers. They take part in both as worthy endeavors unto themselves. One of the common misconceptions about reading and writing is that we bring them together by having students write about what they read, but, in reality, students are writers in their own right. Because they are writers, they read. Professional writers read. In order to become better writers, in addition to writing, the next most important thing writers do is read. Don Murray (1999) says:

> writers have to be readers—skillful readers of their own evolving drafts and insightful readers of the masters who can teach them how to develop their craft. (44)

So, we learned. A classroom of writers reads. They read their own writing while they write, they read one another's writing, and they read the writing of writers beyond their classroom. The writing of professionals extends our students' writing. Reading is the thing to do in a community of writers. Everyone explores the words, worlds, and thoughts of others.

When Tracy's fifth graders studied the textile industry in New England, one of the books several of them enjoyed was *The Bobbin Girl* (McCully 1996). As one student after another read it, seven of them met and talked about how they had read it as writers. One girl took its idea of self-reliance and wrote about the time her soccer team banded together and voiced a concern to their coach. One boy became intrigued by McCully's reference to the looms as "relentless monsters" and wrote a spoof on the looms' refusal to work properly in their determination to make the girls' lives miserable. Someone else, noting the drop in textile prices in McCully's historical fiction, researched the changes in prices over a hundred-year span of time. In *The Bobbin Girl* they found ideas for research, insights into their own lives, and well-crafted phrases. Books keep writers going.

The amount of time students spend engaged in reading sets successful classrooms apart from others (Allington & Cunningham 1996). Engaged readers don't just rattle off words. They find themselves in the midst of what they read. In order for this to happen, especially for students who struggle, the materials they read from cannot be consistently too hard. "Schemes using a single material for all students often create difficulties for lower-achieving readers" (118). Readers do not readily engage in difficult materials, especially students who have yet to become skillful readers. In order to become proficient, readers devote time to reading from books they want to read that are within their reach. They can learn to read these books.

Time to Talk Janine Chappell Carr (1996) wrote about the importance of friends to the children in her first grade when she told Lee's story. Lee, a little waif who had experienced more loss than "any six-year-old should have to," talked with her friends about the loss of her parents and pets. They knew. Some of them had experienced similar grief. Their response to her small words kept Lee going as a reader and writer.

When researchers ask professional writers for additional insights into what helps them become better writers, they say, "Response." Writers seek response at various times during their writing process. Talking helps both the writer and the reader, who searches for value in others' writing, whether it is written by a professional, a classmate, or the teacher.

Variations of the earlier classroom scene with *The Bobbin Girl* occur when small groups meet to talk about their own writing. These pieces of writing are treasure chests waiting for explorers. The responders find well-penned words, significant thoughts, and connections among pieces of writing. The writers learn what is noteworthy in their writing. When Maryanne read her draft about her first lost tooth, the other children commented on her tears.

One child said, "You cried."

Shawn added, "It's just like Madeline because they cry." This talk about their own experiences and those of their favorite characters in literature validated the writer.

These responders told the writer what they valued in her writing, and she, in turn, became increasingly able to find worth in her writing as well as in that of others. Teachers teach their writers to recognize good aspects of writing, whether they note specific words, important ties to other research, or lessons about human worth. They talk about what each person finds in the writing. They often teach mini-lessons on the various treasures found in pieces of writing.

Responders also give specific help if the writer requests it. Sometimes this talk, when it involves a strategy that others may appreciate, extends beyond the response into a lesson. When Bryan needed help with the letter he wanted to write in his search for the prices of textiles, a series of mini-lessons on business letters, part of the fifth-grade curriculum, became part of the next week's agenda. When someone needed help with quotation marks, a child who knew this skill taught it. This kind of talk is meaningful, direct instruction, focused on what the writers need, and they know it is relevant.

Time to Listen Audiences who will respond listen to the authors' voices when they read. They can sense when an author feels confident and when an author is uncertain. These responders, who are writers, are super-tuned-in to whatever and whomever they hear. Nuances in a neighbor's voice and the difference between "reckless monsters" and "undependable looms" impress them. Writers sense when it is appropriate to tell a writer only what sounds clear or when to push. Writer-teachers listen for the insecurity and confidence that permeate the words of the writers in their class.

These teachers can hear a writer when they read the writer's work, even if the writer isn't present. This happens when we have set aside lots of time to hear their real voices and to strengthen those voices so they can resound in their writing. Writers know, instinctively, that their voices reveal themselves to others. If not, why would we be so afraid to read our writing aloud?

When writers do sit on the Author's Chair, they feel the heady feeling of all eyes and ears upon them. To be in that spot is no small thing, which, of course, is why it's so important for the listeners to have rehearsed their role, to take it seriously, and to play it right. They listen for specifics and quote back to the writer what they hear. A listener can't get by with saying, "I liked it." That's the kind of comment a nonlistener can make. When students can get by with that kind of comment, they can get by with not listening.

When they hear specific feedback, writers know their audience listened. When a small child read, "My dad is gone. He moved," no one in Brenda Ross' class said, "I like what you wrote." Someone said, "My dad is gone, too. Where did your dad go?" In no time, the children were talking and listening to one another.

In Victoria Koivu-Rybicki's grade 4 classroom (Madigan & Koivu-Rybicki 1997), the children listen not only to one another but also to themselves. Paul, a child who wrote little all year, emerged in April as a writer who heard his own voice. Throughout the year he talked about one topic, the pervasiveness of crime in his neighborhood and its negative effects on his life. Throughout the year he also dutifully wrote about this topic of his choice in short, perfunctory drafts. Writing down the words he loved to say was very difficult for this lively storyteller who daily engaged in critical thinking.

For months his teacher encouraged Paul's interest and tried to figure out a way for it to bring him into her community of writers. Finally, a suggestion worked. Paul wrote a letter to the director of African American studies at a nearby university, who invited Paul to his center. Paul's excitement now carried him into the world of writers and he ended the year with a long, detailed piece of writing, "Enslaved," which he read to his class. Later, when asked about his journey as a writer, Paul gave an extensive answer ending with, "*You* give yourself ideas and not the teacher!"

It took Paul months to believe in himself enough to write about something he cared deeply about. Writing every day in a classroom in which his teacher and classmates listened carefully to his ideas finally gave him the confidence he needed to become a writer.

It Takes Time to Learn to Question

Questioning others and self is necessary. The most common type of question I hear in reading-writing classrooms is one where the questioner wants to know about the subject at hand. When Fred wrote about his dad's car racing, the other second graders wanted to know, "How fast does his car go?" When a teacher in my class wrote about the advantages of small schools, another teacher in the class wanted to know, "What determines the label 'small school'?" These are straightforward questions the questioner thinks the author knows. There is no hidden agenda. The author is the authority, and he speaks.

Similarly, when a writer shares a book written by a professional, the class expects her to know the book. She tells them something about the book, reads a passage, and invites questions: "What else would you like to know?" In one class, Marcio wanted to know in what year the Bobbin Girl probably worked in the Lowell mills. Ernestina, the girl who shared the book, wasn't sure, but she knew where the information could be found. In no time she had scanned the author's note at the end of the book and provided the answer, "1835." Tracy Belman asked what else happened at that time. They talked.

In preparation for these sessions, writers and readers ask themselves questions. Writers try to answer readers' possible questions as they write, and readers, accustomed to hearing many questions about books, try to anticipate those they will be asked. They become aware of where authors place information. Emily Arnold McCully included some facts within the text of *The Bobbin Girl* and others in her author's note at the end. Students love to write author's notes. As they become aware of what writers and readers do, students consider these new types of writing when they plan for their own growth.

The students and teachers in the research projects I worked on created, over a period of years, five questions that give students the confidence to say, "Yes, I know I'm becoming a better reader-writer." The questions are:

1. What do I know as a reader-writer?
2. What have I recently learned as a reader-writer?
3. What do I want to learn next?
4. What do I plan to do to learn that?
5. What will I put in my portfolio to document that I've learned something new?

These five questions represent a significant part of what I have learned in the twelve years since I wrote the original *When Writers Read*. At that time I didn't realize the importance of *students' questions of themselves* as vehicles that prompted conscious, purposeful growth.

The sequence places the emphasis on what each person knows, on what each person can do. Finessing the way students spend their time so they see themselves as persons who know something and can do things has a tremendous effect on everyone. It is no small thing. It creates magic.

Teachers who have read *When Learners Evaluate* (Hansen 1998b) tell me these questions work for their students, and it usually takes time for students to be able to answer them effectively. Teachers set the questions in motion in various ways. Many listen for an instance when a child—maybe one who sometimes has difficulties—shows his expertise and then introduce the questions to the class at that time.

Ellen Blanchard, who teaches in Rochester, New Hampshire, said to her students one day, "Today PJ read his draft to us about playing ball and told us about how he and his dad practice. He knows a lot, and here are five questions he can use to help him continue with his writing and reading. Some of the rest of you will want to use them also."

PJ answered the questions with the guidance of Ellen as part of an all-class series of mini-lessons. They began, "What do I know as a writer-reader?"

PJ knew how to read his own drafts, could draw lots of things, and could write about his family. For his formal answer to the question, he wrote, "I know how to write about my family and I can read it to everyone."

Some students, as these questions become more widely used, begin to interpret the question "What do I know?" in a variety of ways, including what they know about the process of writing and about various skills. They know how to replace passive verbs with active ones and how to add characters' thoughts to their writing, for example.

For question two, "What have I recently learned as a reader-writer?," PJ considered with the class a few options. He could list some words he had recently learned to spell, the information he learned about bobcats from Shawn's writing, or that he could answer questions the class asked him. He wrote, "About bobcats from Shawn."

For question three, "What do I want to learn next?", PJ also had several possibilities, but when it came time to choose the one to write in his portfolio, suspense entered the scene. PJ rose, went to the bookshelf, and returned with Shawn's latest book, *The Tiger I Saw and Facts About Tigers*. PJ wrote, "I want to learn to read Shawn's *Tiger* book."

The next question, "What do I plan to do to learn that?," can become complicated. Often, a student needs to do several things in order to accomplish the goal he stated in response to the third question. In this case, after discussing possibilities, PJ created this plan: "(1) Shawn will read it to me. (2) We will read it together lots. (3) I will read it at home. (4) I will read it alone."

Finally, "What will I put in my portfolio to document that I've learned something new?" This question became PJ's opportunity to provide evidence of his growth. His successive entries showed what he could do, that he was a learner, a reader, a writer. PJ created a chart of what he did each day for five days to learn to read Shawn's book. And he photocopied one page from the book—the hardest page.

Prior to the initiation of these five questions, upon consultation with Kathy Staley, the school's reading teacher, Ellen and the children brought items from home to answer the question "Who am I?" They wrote about these, put them in their portfolios, and shared them. On the day PJ shared information about playing ball with his dad he became a member of the class. The other children did not know that this child who hung on the sidelines could throw and catch. "You play ball?" they asked. They brought PJ into their play that very morning at recess, he gained status, and his confidence allowed him to learn.

Ellen, seizing upon this momentous occasion, introduced the five questions into their classroom routine. Now the children can systematically move forward and document their journeys. She, in turn, provides time for them to work, each day, on their goals. Their own questions set them up for a lifetime as learners, readers, and writers.

Hmmmm . . .

Time. The *when* of it all, as a friend of mine calls it.

Both teachers and students fuss about when to do what. Making their own decisions about the use of their time is a hugely important part of what writers and readers do, regardless of age. To teach our students how to make increasingly better decisions about the use of their time is a significant aspect of what we do as literacy teachers. We create an overall structure, and our students determine for themselves how they will spend their time along the way as they work on their various reading-writing tasks.

When we design the general framework within which our students will work, we consider everything from our own personal quirks, to the makeup of our class(es), to the pressure we feel from frameworks and standards, to maybe ten other factors. Our structure reflects our values and sometimes reveals our panic-stricken state of being. Part of our desperation comes from a lack of knowledge about ways to use time. Last Saturday I lunched with a former intern of mine who is now a grades 5/6 teacher. Lauren said, "Jane, I didn't learn in any of my classes in grad school how to design a school day. I just don't know how to do it. There isn't time for everything. That I do know for sure."

Streamlining our days is one way to see time as an ally rather than a foe. Lauren and I brainstormed ways for her to do this, and I relearned the importance of idiosyncrasies. Lauren's situation is different from most other teachers, so everyone needs to find his own solution, but we based our brainstorm on Lauren's conviction that she had to create as few blocks of time as possible. Having large blocks of time in which to learn is something Lauren now knows is necessary for her students.

They have four basic subjects: math, science, social studies, and language arts. Their specials are all in the time block before lunch every day, so they have from 9:00 to 11:30 A.M. and 1:30 to 3:30 P.M. for their four core subjects. Lauren sees it as doable to teach math and science for an hour each every afternoon. Her district has kits for science that circulate among the teachers, and this year they created their own math curriculum. Lauren and a friend swap students for these two subjects. One of them teaches all the math and the other all the science. Whew! The afternoon fell into place easily.

The morning we never did figure out. Lauren loves social studies. When she served as my intern she turned her classroom into a campfire ring with a fire in the center, logs to sit on, and trees to surround it. So, she had been dividing the morning into one and half hours for social studies and one hour for language arts, but that wasn't working at all. One hour was just not enough time for writing, reading, grammar, spelling, and the odds and ends of other language arts–related requirements.

The easy solution would be to flip-flop the language arts hour with the one and a half hours of social studies, but Lauren did not want to give up any of the time she had set aside her first love. What she wanted to do was combine language arts and social studies, but she worried about her students' personal reading and writing. When would they have time to read the information and books they craved that were unrelated to social studies? When would they have time to write letters to the librarian to thank her for the new shipment of books or any other writing they wanted to do that was unrelated to social studies?

Somehow, she decided within a two-and-a-half-hour block for social studies and language arts, a general work time could provide students with time to read and write for their own purposes and for the purposes of social studies. This could give the students valuable practice on time management; they didn't need to indulge in both kinds of reading every day, but they did need to do so within extended periods of time. In addition, within the large block of time, a time for mini-lessons or maxi-lessons could give Lauren and the students opportunities to teach whatever appeared to be the main issue(s) of the day, whether it be predominantly social studies or language arts.

The overall time schedule would guarantee time for students to share both their own reading-writing and their social studies work in small groups and with the class.

It all sounds much clearer today than it did when Lauren and I talked, and she kept saying things like, "But on Fridays several of my students leave for instrumental music lessons, so I have to consider that, and on this other day. . . ." Interruptions. Finding large blocks of time is like finding large blocks of gold in the central office. Unbelievable treasures.

Response,
Response-ability,
Responsibility

Six

When Liberty decided that her draft about the school fair was
ready to go into the class newsletter, she announced from the
Author's Chair, "This is my article for the newsletter, and it's
done. When I finish reading it to you, I want you to tell me what
you think is the most interesting piece of news in it." She read
and several hands went up.

The first student to respond said, "Hands down, the notes. I
had no idea the messengers delivered eighty-two!"

"To me, the most interesting news was . . . ," added another
student, and on it went.

They gave Liberty the response she requested. The sixth-grade
teachers at Stratham say their students share for this type of cel-
ebratory response more than any other. Response supported this
writer-reader's confidence in her ability to make decisions.
Writing and reading aren't formulaic. There was no rule to tell
Liberty what to include in her article, but she felt she had made
wise decisions. Regardless, she wanted to know which news bits
struck her readers as noteworthy.

On another day around the Author's Chair, Nathaniel read a
draft about the students' first-grade reading buddies. He was not
finished and requested examples of "funny things that have happened when you were with your buddy." He heard several and
chose a couple to write into his draft.

On a third day, Angela read aloud from a book she was in the
midst of, *The Watsons Go to Birmingham—1963* (Curtis 1995).
She had never before heard about the bombing of the church and

was confused. Several students had already read this book and carefully tried to explain this difficult event to her.

These students purposely use occasions to share as opportunities to move their writing and reading forward or to learn about the impact of their work. They plan ahead and take advantage of their time in the Author's Chair, which is very different from situations in which students in years past read drafts, and classmates, without guidance from the presenter, offered suggestions such as "I think you should. . . ." These kinds of evaluations by others, we now know, can undercut the writer's own evaluation of her work. She quickly thinks that to evaluate herself is not her responsibility, that evaluation rests in the hands of others. Unfortunately, this kind of thinking does little to help the person see herself as an independent learner.

Sometimes the student who shares seeks open response. As Pete settled into the chair he said, "Anything goes, folks. When I finish, tell me what you like, ask me questions, give me suggestions, anything. Ready?" He read and they did offer him a potpourri of response, which is what he wanted, and he later sorted through it as he shaped his draft.

Readers and Writers Seek Response

Seeking response is natural. The ultimate learners are tiny children who begin to make sense of an ultraconfusing world the second they burst forth into it. They respond to touch, love, and the souls of those who provide warmth. These small beings hear words, eventually sort out what they mean, and learn how to use words to get the attention and needs they deem important.

They ask zillions of questions as they use language to help them figure out things. But, children vary tremendously when we look at what they wonder about, whom they ask questions of, and how assertive they are. The people around them inadvertently show toddlers the family's ways of finding out about their world. Some families work together, some limit their inquiries, and some explore everywhere. Some use many words, some use many crayons, and some use little of either.

Inquiry is an act of imposition (Lindfors 1999), and children learn how to impose. Some live life straight on, and others circle around. Some ask questions directly, and others tell you stories, expecting you to respond with yours.

Students seek response around the Author's Chair, in small groups, in conferences with their teacher, and when they interact with others during their workshop time. Often it is from the teacher they seek response. The teacher's role as responder to readers and writers is curious. Whereas her role is to teach, within the teaching of literacy we label this role *response*. The teacher responds to students' requests, to students' needs at any time during the school day; careful acknowledgment of others is a way of life. Often students seek attention at unexpected moments.

Jill Ostrow (1998) wrote about her multiage, grades 4–6 classroom and her insistence on the students' continuous respect for one another. When one boy said, "I'm not sittin' by no girl!" Jill knew he was seeking attention, but from her he received none at that moment. She leaned back in her chair, wondering what the class would say. The others called the boy on the inappropriateness of his comment, and Jill led them as they all worked, throughout the year, on their interactions with one another.

Evan, a fifth grader at the Stratham elementary school, wanted the overall response he was receiving to change. As a student who went to the resource room for part of his day, he burned under the scorn of some of the boys in his classroom. But, in writing, he found his niche. He loved to write poems and shared them regularly with the class during October. At the end of the month he read the following poem:

Halloween

Ghosts and goblins.
Howling wolves.
Crying cats.
Witches on brooms
with green hair
flying through the air.
Little children
yelling, "Trick or treat!"

His classmates were in awe of his poetry, but they were confused. After all, he went to the resource room. They didn't expect this of him, but his poems did start to temper their teasing. Further, Chad and Lester wondered how to cast him in a story they were writing. They thought he should be the wizard, but, "It's kind of weird for Evan to be a wizard," Lester said.

"He doesn't have much power. He's a beginner," Chad said.

Later, as the two boys continued to write, they turned to me and explained, "Evan's the dumbo in this story. He's not a dumbo really, but he is in this story. Sometimes he is, a little, like when he laughs." They turned to nearby Evan and said, "Evan, laugh."

Evan emitted a weird laugh. He performed, but I feared he hated this light teasing. This was kindness, however, compared to how Chad used to tease Evan. The tone had started to change; Evan noticed the difference, and wanted his situation to improve even more. He had started to see himself as someone with potential.

Evan wanted to get out of the resource room. He refused to listen to the social studies tapes they provided to accompany his classroom text. He gutted his way through the book. Evan wanted to write his entries in his reading notebook to his grade 5 teacher, not to the resource room adults. He wanted to become more involved in his classroom. Evan relished the positive response he received when he read his poetry to the class and wanted to do something to ensure this tone in other situations.

He wrote a book for his classmates:

How to Write Poems

First	Look around the classroom Get ideas
Second	Read some poetry
Third	Write down things
Fourth	Share with friends and get ideas
Fifth	Elaborate them Share with classroom Get more ideas
Sixth	Elaborate more and write more poems Then publish
Seventh	Make sure you have pictures
Eighth	Make sure you leave extra pages so you can put more poems in back of book

With this special invitation, he hoped others would be more inclined to seek help from him with their poetry, and they were. This impact of his writing was important to Evan but, more importantly, he had found a way to shine, to hold a needed position in his community. This is what Evan sought, crafted, and eventually received. Inclusion became the overall response pattern of his classmates.

Readers and Writers Respond to Others

We base response on the assumption that the writer wants to go back to work. In order for students to be able to respond in supportive ways when a reader-writer seeks no specific response, teachers teach various possibilities.

I will show various options for response to one example, a draft of a poem written by Devon, a second-grade boy in Mast Way School in New Hampshire. All of these options would probably never occur as responses to one piece of writing, but they are all possibilities teachers consider when they look at the overall types of response they want to occur in their classrooms.

Hockey

Hockey is a winter sport.
It needs ice to move.
When you skate,
ice chips fly behind you.
Swish, swish, swish,
your skates move along the ice
while you handle the heavy rubber puck.
Swosh, swosh, swosh,
your skates are picking up speed
while you skate across the blue line.
You pass to your team mate.
He skates across the red line.
We're half way to the goal.
Swash, swash, swash,
you're almost full speed
when you're crossing the opposite blue line.
Swip, swip, swip,
you're full speed.
While you're in the circle
your stick goes back.
You shoot
and score!

Responding to Content At the end of his reading to the class, Devon said aloud, "I play hockey, and I know how to move the puck fast." It's quite natural for a writer to make a comment about his own work, sort of as a postscript. He wants to make sure his audience gets it.

The first person to comment picked up on what Devon started. He emphasized the content of his poem, and the child who spoke did likewise, "And you know the sounds of hockey!" A different response from a class member or teacher might have been, "You sure do know how to move it fast!" This would have been more specifically related to what Devon had said. Regardless, responding to the content is often a starting place in response. Authors write to deliver information, and they want their message to come through.

If this had been a poem written by a professional writer and read to the class by Devon, his comment to open the discussion might have been exactly the same, "I play hockey, and I know how to move the puck fast." The first response from the class might have been questions about Devon's playing or confirmation about what he did. Eventually, however, they would return to the text. If not, the teacher would do so by entering into the discussion: "You know, Devon, in that poem you read, the author created great sounds. Could you read them again?"

Responding with Connections to Life Experiences Devon could have offered the following as his first comment after reading his poem to his classmates: "I'm in the Spurts League." He didn't say this in his poem, but he could have added this information after the reading. If he had, children might have immediately responded with information about their leagues and teams. However, eventually they would return to Devon's poem to talk specifically about the worth of some of his exact words. Returning to the author's work is crucial. I have been in a few situations where response never focused on the student's piece of writing, and the writer invariably expressed concern at some later time.

An alternative scene for Devon's sharing could have been a conference with his teacher. He could have offered his "I'm in the Spurts League" comment and she might have responded with questions about his league. Maybe she would have added, "I might go to a game sometime." If she were to go, she would verify the importance of the students' outside lives to their classroom work.

Responding to the Use of Language It is always good to point out specific words to a writer, words that have stayed with you. Writers appreciate knowing which words are effective. Often responders ask the writer, "What specific words are you glad you used?"

Devon could have replied, "I used good action words! I changed from *swish,* to *swosh,* to *swash,* to *swip* when he scored." These occasions for self-evaluation give the writer opportunities to congratulate himself amidst others who appreciate his skill.

"Yes, they're great action words. How'd you make 'em up?"

The conversation would then continue.

Similar conversations focus on the use of language when students share the writing of professionals. Writers love words, and finding the right one can be as exciting as finding the right piece for a thousand-piece puzzle.

Responding to the Writing Process Used Trish Sutphen, Devon's teacher, knew how this poem came to be, wanted the class to know, and therefore requested, "Could you tell everyone how you started to write this?"

Devon said, "This is the first time I saw pictures in my mind before I wrote something."

"What do you mean?" asks someone.

Devon reminded the class of the recent occasion when Trish had read them a poem, asked them to picture it in their minds, and suggested they create pictures on manila paper. Instead, Devon had created his poem at that time. The children were intrigued with this new way to go about writing, by starting with pictures in your mind. As writers, they were interested in variations of the writing process that their classmates used in particular situations.

Trish added, "And this is the first time you wrote an entire piece of writing with such enthusiasm in one sitting." This writing process had worked, and it might for someone else. They all knew that their writing processes differed from one another's and differed in various situations.

Responding to the Effect of the Writing on Readers Devon might have said, "I think people can picture the ice chips flying. People who don't know about hockey will know how fast we skate."

"Right, it's easy to picture the ice flying behind you. It goes off like this," a speaker might have responded, flinging his arms to the side while confirming Devon's thought about the impact of his poem. Writers want assurance that their writing can affect others. The purpose of much writing is to get response. It's supposed to make a difference. When writers feel this potential, they get a heady feeling that allows them to take off.

Similarly, if this poem had been written by a professional, and someone read it to the class, the listeners might have responded to its effect on them. For example, "It made me feel excited, like when I score in soccer!"

Responding to the Use of Conventions In an editing conference, Devon said, "I used periods and commas."

His teacher responded, "Excellent. You did. The commas between the sound words are especially helpful to the reader. So, let's see. You do have some capitals that need to be fixed. Whom could you go to?" They agreed on two possible student-helpers, and Devon was off.

This corresponds to a situation in which another student in the class was practicing so he could read Devon's poem to his buddy in a different classroom. "I can read all the regular words without it sounding choppy, but I can't keep *swish*, *swosh*, and *swash* apart," he said.

These are straightforward short vowel sounds, but in this context the reader needed to have this pointed out to him. He didn't appear to have the necessary meta-awareness of his short vowels. An extremely brief, on-the-spot lesson from his teacher clarified these sounds and this reader was prepared.

Responding to Requests "I would like to know how to shape this on a page," is a request Devon made at one point. He knew what he wanted to work on.

"OK, we can work on that," Trish responded. When her students are engaged in their writing and reading she seldom has a chance to wonder, "What should I teach?" They seek constant teaching from her—direct instruction, on the spot, while they are in the process of writing and reading. These students see themselves with potential, see themselves with a future, and intend to direct that future.

Frequently, Devon's teacher takes one request and turns it into a mini-lesson, as she did with this opportunity. Devon showed the class his earlier, unshaped poem, and the shape I have used here, his final shape, for comparison. On three successive days, three other students put drafts of poems on overhead projector transparencies for the class to help them reshape. Typically, mini-lessons come in a series that all focus on one topic, such as the shapes of poems. Most writing and reading strategies are too complicated to learn in one brief lesson.

The scene for Devon's request could have been different. He might have asked the class rather than the teacher for a particular kind of help. These requests need to be handled with care. Sometimes classmates become overzealous in their helpfulness. Probably three suggestions is plenty. This gives the writer enough options without overloading him with possibilities.

It is important to keep in mind that suggestions to a writer come in response to a specific request from the writer. The writer evaluates his work, finds a need, and asks for help. Respondents seldom step in with unsolicited suggestions.

Responding with Possible Future Writing in Mind   It is quite common for students to want to know one another's plans. Later on in the class discussion, a student asked, "What are you going to write next?"

Devon said, "I could write a poem about each game we won."

"Yes," responded another, "and you could write about how you learned to play."

"Or, about practice."

Writers write and they are always looking ahead. Devon's idea to write a series of poems about each game might have prompted someone else to write a series about each of his cousins or about every recess for a week. Writers are always on the alert for ideas.

If this had been a poem written by a professional, and Devon had read it to the class, someone might have asked a similar question at some point in the discussion, such as "What are you going to read next?" Readers, as well as writers, plan ahead.

Responding to Connections with Other Students   In a small group, Devon, still thinking about what he might do next, said, "I could talk to Bud and write about a time he and I took the puck all the way down the rink."

Bud jumped at the chance to do this, and they made a few quick plans. When students bring up the possibility of working with others, their teachers typically try to facilitate these connections and even encourage others. Sometimes, of course, learners need to work alone, but the intermingling helps them see one another as writers and readers. Writing and reading are cool tasks to be involved in, and the teacher tries to promote this camaraderie, this sense that writing and reading are the things to do here.

When everyone is involved, response happens all around us, all the time. Kathy Perfect (1999) wrote about how important it is for her to constantly seek and value her students' thoughts about poetry. This determines their confidence in their ability to read poetry and keeps them engaged.

Readers and Writers Reflect

How to respond to all of her little children's needs became problematic for Brenda Jentes, a first-grade teacher in Manchester. She talked about this when she spoke at a National Council of Teachers of English conference. "I was so gushy. I said, 'That's wonderful!' 'Oh, you're so special!' 'Oooh, your picture is sooo pretty!' 'That's wonderful!' all day long. Somehow, I thought that by constantly telling my little children that they were wonderful, they would not need me so much.

"But then one day, Cindy, the researcher who works in my classroom, and I were having one of our intense, heart-to-heart talks. We just love our children and we want so much for them to do well. Our conversation was about evaluation, the topic of our research. Everyone in our project wants to teach their students to evaluate themselves. The other classrooms in the project are of older students, but we are determined to teach our children to be able to say exactly what is good about a piece of their own writing.

"So, we decided to model for them. When we started to carefully monitor our words, we both heard ourselves saying, 'Oh, this is wonderful! This is great! I just love this! This is wonderful!' all day long. We weren't telling the children what they were doing well. Then, when we wanted them to tell us why they chose items for their portfolios, we wondered why they always said, 'I chose this because it's good.'

"We changed right away, but do you know how hard it is to stop telling children they are wonderful? But I had to. They couldn't evaluate themselves after my gushes. I needed to be quiet and say, 'Tell me about this.'

"'It's about my gramma.'"

"'Oh, tell me about her.'"

"'She lives with us.'"

"'She does? I used to live with my gramma. Please read it to me.'"

"The child reads her line of print and tells me about her picture. I sense she loves to feel her gramma's cat purr and notice she has tried to write a word for this sound. The children love to represent sounds, and this is the first time Camille has tried to do so. Not surprising, she points to *pR* when I ask for her favorite word. She can evaluate her work.

"I tell her I am impressed by how well she wrote the special sound her gramma's cat makes when she's content. Camille and the other children devote longer and longer lengths of time to their writing when they know we all will quietly respond to their self-acknowledged, specific, forward strides."

Brenda's reflection caused her to change and set the stage for her students to think more carefully about themselves.

Reflecting Through Art   Kathy Staley studies the role reflection plays in the lives of teacher educators who, in turn, advocate reflection. Kathy, a visual artist, studies teacher educators who aren't artists, but who have placed themselves in positions where they experience the power of the arts for themselves and their students. For some, their ability to find value in their own work occurs most readily when they use art as their mode of reflection.

One of the teacher educators Kathy has studied uses collage to reveal relationships among various aspects of his self. Dan began his consideration of art when he enrolled in one of my classes. I required the students to create three, two-part answers to the question "Who am I as a learner?" One part of each answer was to be in writing and the other part was to be shown via the visual arts, music, or performance.

Dan's three answers showed him as a learner who has an adventurous spirit, who has grown as a teacher, and who is constantly learning to be a parent of three children. For his entry about his adventurous spirit, he wrote a poem and created a collage (see Figure 6-1) that became a turning point for him. His depiction of exploration in Australia guided him as he kept his spirit alive. It appeared before his mind with more clarity than only a poem, and he is a published poet. His collage helped him focus on what he wanted to cultivate in himself.

Dan realized, for the first time, the significance of the visual arts to him. He now requires all of his students to create visuals for at least one assignment. Some gain a newfound appreciation for the arts and some closet artists sigh huge sighs of thankfulness. Few teachers have sought those students' preferred mode of expression, and Dan encourages them to continue to create visuals whenever an assignment provides space for them to make decisions about its form, and many assignments do.

One of the ways I introduce visual response to the students in my university class of K–12 teachers is for all of us to create visual responses to Tomi dePaola's *The Art Lesson* (1989). We have the best time! Each table shares a box of sixty-four crayons, per the book, and we use all kinds of paper. When we go around the

Darwin
TROPIC OF CAPRICORN
AUSTRALIA
Perth
Sydney
Route: part one
College years are ones
where students come
to find their way and their voice.
If I am successful as a teacher,
I will have inspired some of them
to see possibilities in themselves
that they otherwise might not have seen.
RAMBLES
MANFORD

Figure 6-1. Dan's adventurous spirit.

class to share, we see cartoons, line drawings of our own school experiences, and shaded still scenes of fall vegetables. Our own art lesson shows the richness of variety, and our interpretations of this book become larger and deeper. We see it in new ways.

Open Invitations for Reflections An open invitation to respond to a piece of writing with your own thoughts often brings unexpected reflections. When Meg Floyd's first-grade daughter read aloud her homework story about young children who tease an overweight girl, Meg squirmed. Finally, when her daughter finished, Meg issued an open invitation: "What do you think this story is about?"

"It's about a girl who's fat and when she loses weight she'll have friends."

Meg became oh-so-scared about this message and talked to her daughter's teacher. This wise teacher instituted children's response to stories the very next day, a practice she had never before employed. She had always guided the children's responses to assigned stories, and for this story, in previous years, she had led them in a discussion about tolerance of difference. However, when she sought the children's own response, an entirely different discussion arose, of the type she continued to learn about in *Mosaic of Thought* (Keene & Zimmerman 1997). She wanted to hear the children's own thoughts and to be part of discussions of their viewpoints.

We want children to reflect on what they read, rather than reflect on the messages we think their stories contain. We learn a great deal, and so do our students, when their reflections set the agenda for our instruction. When we seek their responses as primary we help them see their own thoughts as worthy.

Hmmmm . . .

Pat McLure's first-grade children raise chicks in the spring and invite other classes to their room to view them. Their guests love the babies in the incubator, and Pat's children proudly tell their visitors anything they want to know about their offspring. They have immersed themselves in a study of chicks and willingly dispense their expertise.

One day after visits by a second grade and a fourth grade, Pat called her class together to reflect on these visitations. "What did you learn from our guests?" she began.

Of the various comments, one struck me the most: "Second graders are smarter than fourth graders."

"Why do you say that?" Pat wondered.

"They asked more questions!"

When it comes to response, these little children cherish questions. The more queries, the more interested their visitors evidently are. I learned about this importance of questions when Pat asked her children to reflect upon their experiences.

Setting aside time to reflect on visitations, reading groups, writing conferences, or other classroom experiences provides the teachers with information, tells students how much their teacher values their thoughts, and shows them the importance of reflection. Teachers set aside time to think back on what has happened. Experiences gain value when our students' thoughts inform us about an event.

Self-Discipline |

Seven

If there's one outstanding characteristic of writers, it's *self-discipline*. Writers write no matter what. I mean, you can do everything you can think of to get them away from their writing, but you'll rarely succeed.

Writers know that writing is hard. Very hard. They know that some days their writing will not get far, but they put in their time. They put words on the page, even if the words don't thrill them. However, and thankfully, words sparkle forth on other days. Not knowing what kind of day lies ahead, the writer always writes. She doesn't dare miss what might be a terrific day, but to be so consistent is not easy. She has a structure for her days that preserves a space for writing, and whether she follows it depends on the strength of her self-discipline.

In my own case, I am the one, for the most part, who structures my life, my writing, and my reading. My self-discipline tends to keep me on task and ensures I use the spaces I reserve. The hard part is deciding how many spaces to reserve and how large each one needs to be—or how small.

Writing and reading aren't my life. I know I need spaces in which to walk, to prepare dinner, to eat three meals, to be with friends, to be a family member, to appreciate my students, to re-search, *and* to read and write. My list is too long, but it shows what I value.

I learned from Don Graves to program time for research into my academic life. I do this in various ways at various times. Over the years, I have typically set aside two days per week for my re-search, and this works for me. When someone approaches me to schedule a meeting on a Tuesday or a Thursday, I don't even need to open my little black book. I know I'm not available. Most of my colleagues by now know this as well.

Part of being a researcher is to write, and setting aside time to write professionally works for me, but writing in other genres is something I find hard to maintain. For years I've written personal narratives with my classes, and I find the process of learning via writing amazing. I truly came to appreciate one of my grandmothers by writing about her; I'm so very glad I did. I worked on that draft off and on for a few years, as various classes helped me figure out what I was trying to say about her. At the same time, I worked on various other narratives and published the one I excerpted at the beginning of this book. I know my self needs this writing, and I've joined a women's writing group to bolster my self-discipline.

Reading isn't hard, but I'm just never satisfied with the amount of reading I do. I'm in the midst of *Mother of Pearl*, by Melinda Haynes (1999), and I'd love to be reading it right now! Teachers in my university classes sometimes say, "I can't read if I have some work I must do, because once I get into a book, I can't put it down and I don't do my work." Well, I do have enough self-discipline to put down the book and do my work, which at this moment is to write this book, but I just don't seem to be able to figure out how to hold sacred enough space to feel satisfied with myself as a reader of adult literature, children's literature, professional books, and journals. I constantly struggle with all these kinds of reading I want to do.

I interact with many people each day and lots of them have values different from mine. They request pieces of my self, and I have to make decisions. At other times, my own tasks want to creep into other spaces, and my disciplined voice says, "No, I can't do this now. It's time to take a walk." The frequency of a routine gives me enough experience with walking or writing or whatever to know I want to do it.

Similarly, students keep themselves engaged when we schedule regular time for them to read and write, stretch their ability to make decisions, and respond to their needs. Many become swept into their joys and preserve reading and writing for themselves.

Relationships Beget Self-Discipline

An important part of reading is talk. Readers jabber about books. Joan Von Dras (1995) wrote about the positive influence on her class when her students started to relate the interactions among the characters in the books they discussed to their own behavior, a type of conversation they eventually could handle without her presence. They challenged and supported one another's behavior and learned to monitor their interactions.

In order for talk about books to thrive, many teachers teach their students to use the same structure they use when they talk about their own writing. It doesn't matter what the structure is, as long as students respond to all writers—their classmates, selves, teacher, and professionals—with similar respect. I hear many different examples in various teachers' classrooms.

Phyllis Kinzie initially teaches her fourth graders to respond to one another's drafts with this simple procedure: "I remember . . ." and "I'd love to know more about. . . ." For "I remember . . . ," the responder quotes something he remembers from the draft. For "I'd love to know more about . . . ," the responder seeks more information such as how often the author eats at fast-food joints, how it feels to live half years with a father in Hawaii, or whatever. Responders seek information beyond what they learn from a draft itself.

Phyllis' students use this same format for reading. They meet in clusters to respond to one another's books of choice and come prepared. Each reader begins his turn by reading a portion aloud from the book he is reading, something he values, wants to share, which is akin to "I remember. . . ." Then that student says, "I'd love to know more about . . . ," and proceeds to wonder about something in the book he is reading. Readers wonder why characters do what they do, why people say what they say, and mention whatever piques their curiosity in their book. This serves as a conversation starter to draw others into their book and generates sincere wondering, stimulated by the reader. These students don't meet to answer comprehension questions posed by their teacher. They meet to talk with one another about issues they identify.

Some students meet in reading-writing groups, different from reading or writing groups. They share and respond to both their own writing and that of professionals in one sitting. A student shares similarities between his own writing and what he reads in children's literature. Much learning from writers about writing and reading occurs. Gradually students become aware of the power of their conversations and begin to push one another forward.

Nancy Herdecker, who taught fourth grade in Stratham, heard the following challenge and came into the teachers room excited. Paul, a student who had been in her classroom for only three days, had just met for his first time with a group of children to discuss the books they were reading (Hansen 1992a). In his former school, students never did this.

Two children in the group shared, the children discussed each of those books, and then the third person said, "I don't have anything to share."

Paul was next and appeared to take relief from the previous student's out. Paul said, "I don't have anything either."

David tried to bring Paul in. He pointed to the book in Paul's lap and said, "Share that. Just share a part."

Paul asked if he could get a different book, which he did, and then shared it.

David had sensed how much he could challenge Paul and issued him the pressured invitation. His insistence assured Paul that his groupmates were truly interested in what he had read. An overall belief in the value of each person permeated this classroom. They were not in competition. They worked together. Each brought a different book and the others wanted to know about it. More importantly, each child knew how important it was for each of them to be in the spotlight. They knew Paul needed to experience their support in order to become a reader. Then his own desire could give him the self-discipline to keep himself engaged.

Meaningful Tasks Beget Self-Discipline

When little David, a first grader in Manchester, brought from home a birthday card his dad had created and sent from prison "because he can't go shopping to buy one," David began to create his classroom identity. When his teacher encouraged him during writing to create cards for his dad, David's self found a space in school. His teacher honored who he was.

This small step is huge. Being able to bring their selves into their classrooms enables students to create spaces for themselves (Saez 1995). Their school lives include them. They do not have to draw lines between who they are and what they do in school. Writing for children like David becomes real.

The bringing in of artifacts enlarges the possibilities for writing in classrooms where students have always had choice. When the Manchester students bring artifacts, they bring reality in and consider types of writing they have not extensively used in school. They now realize the importance of information they have not previously considered in their classrooms.

The process of setting a goal to create and send four cards put David in a position where self-discipline entered his school life. This young child knew, intuitively, what he needed. With a well-carved work schedule and access to guidance, his own interest provided the self-discipline he needed to pursue his goal without someone to nag him.

When the Manchester students showed us how important it was for them to bring their selves into the classrooms, I started to see classrooms anew (Hansen 1992b). This was more than "choose your own topic" or "choose your own book." Their self-evaluations placed them in a position to determine what in their lives they valued and, when honored in their classrooms, those interests enabled them to discipline themselves, to keep themselves on task.

The task of their teachers was no longer to motivate the students. Instead, they created the overall situation in which the children pursued tasks they saw as worthwhile. Writing and reading became times when students created spaces in which they saw themselves as readers and writers.

David started to plan ahead. When faced with his daily decision of which to do first after recess, read or write, he now chose to write. In the midst of cards, he was determined to give them first priority.

Students structured their time so they had opportunities to work on their self-designed tasks. When they brought the literacies of their lives and communities into the classroom, we saw students teaching one another how to create cards, read train schedules, and create brochures. More students wanted to read and write.

Commitment Requires
Self-Discipline

Ellen Blanchard, an experienced grade 3 teacher in New Hampshire, worries about standardized tests. "Jane, my students love to read and write and I fear these new state tests will sap some of their energy," she told me. "And, for other teachers, those who are just beginning to figure out how to create a reading-writing classroom, the tests may lead them off-track, and their students may never love to read and write. Maybe there are some teachers whose students rarely wrote and read, and now, because of the tests, these teachers provide additional opportunities for their students to do so, but I'm not convinced that the tests beget exciting reading-writing classrooms."

Ellen's concerns nagged her, and here's what she did about them: During the first year of the existence of the state tests, Ellen ignored them. Her children wrote every day and she taught them their skills while they were in the process of writing. They loved to write! They read every day from books of their choice and shared books. Ellen taught them their skills while they were in the process of reading, and they loved to read! Then, the test results arrived. Not good. Ellen knew she had to do something. She and her colleagues studied the scores to decide what to do, and Ellen created a plan for the following year.

She selected one low area to work on—the open-ended questions in the reading comprehension test. In order for students to receive high scores, they need to include the questions in their answers. For example, "What team does John want to captain?" must be answered in this way: "John wants to captain the Patriots team." Ellen's children had simply written, "Patriots."

Ellen knew her children could understand what they read and could write about their books, so she chose this section to focus on for higher scores. The low scores gave the impression her students didn't comprehend, and she knew better. She intended to change that misperception. However, she also intended to carefully preserve her readers and writers. They—and she—must not become obsessed with the answers to these questions.

Throughout the next fall her students participated in the regular readers-writers workshops Ellen had created for years. They read and wrote every day, and they talked every day about their writing and reading. Talk was Ellen's focus throughout the fall. They read an array of books, including many of their choice, and they wrote about all sorts of topics within many genres, including notebook entries about their books. Every child wrote one each week, and they wrote responses to one another. Ellen wrote an entry in her *Readers Notebook* every day and exchanged with one child. She wrote a response to the child's entry and the child responded to hers. Writing about books was not Ellen's focus in the fall, but her children did write about what they read.

When the children returned to school in January, Ellen introduced reading comprehension questions. She asked one question each week about the book she was reading to the class. She wrote it on the board and, while they talked about it, each child wrote an answer. Ellen's mini-lessons focused on the state's way to write a good answer. For three weeks Ellen conducted one of those lessons per week.

Then, she said to the class, "Let's brainstorm at least three different ways we can continue to practice this skill once a week until you take the test." Their three ideas were: (1) We kids could think of a question every Wednesday about the book you are reading to us, and everyone can write an answer. (2) We can meet with a partner to talk about the books each of us has chosen and write an answer to one question our partner asks us. (3) We can think of three questions for the book you are reading to us, and we can each choose one to write an answer for. They chose the latter option.

On the day they created the questions, three children, one per question, wrote their answers on an overhead transparency for a class discussion of what the state expects for a good answer.

The children's scores improved and that year Ellen was pleased, but she felt the need to explain the situation she was in "These exercises didn't interfere with their love for reading and writing," she told me. "That was my main goal."

"However, these exercises took time away from other reading and writing, but not much. I kept the atmosphere surrounding this practice cheerful, not stressful, so they didn't look at these lessons in a negative way. The exercises did give them some choice, and they did engage in a bit of writing, which remained a tiny proportion of all the writing they did, so maybe it was just a new genre and was OK. To write these formatted answers, they did need to read the questions carefully and read their answers as they wrote. Maybe that careful reading is good."

Ellen didn't want to make other adjustments, however. This test task violates normal conventions of language use; people don't repeat questions when they answer them. This is not a valid skill for students to learn and represents only one of the many negative features of standardized tests. The two largest organizations in the field of reading-writing have taken stands against standardized tests, but these tests continue to proliferate (NCTE 1999; IRA 1999).

Ellen worries about new teachers who set up classrooms with these tests in mind. They may not yet have well-ingrained values about readers and writers, and the tests may more easily distract them than they have Ellen and her students. Inexperienced teachers may not have the self-discipline necessary to adhere to a schedule in which students read and write print that finds a home deep within their souls and makes a difference.

Mark Milliken, at the time of this next story, was teaching fourth grade at Moharimet School in Madbury, New Hampshire. He also worried about the effect of the state tests on his classroom of readers and writers. His way of addressing his concerns also encompasses two years.

During the first year, 1996–97, Mark decided to explain the state rubric for the writing task and teach his students to use it throughout the year. However, his students couldn't use the rubric. They just couldn't get it; it didn't make sense to them. The language wasn't theirs; they couldn't use it effectively. They couldn't use it to evaluate and improve their drafts.

So, Mark created a new plan for 1997–98. As with Ellen, he devoted the entire fall to the creation of a reading-writing workshop in which his students were engaged in their work. They wrote every day in various genres to learn about topics they chose to pursue, and they read books about these topics and others. They enjoyed finding new information and the special twists writers use to relay their knowledge and tell their stories effectively.

Mark's students liked to write, read, and talk about their work. They regularly and frequently talked about the new writing skills and strategies they were learning from professionals and purposely infused them into their own work. They were writers.

In January, when his students had acquired strong skills as evaluators of their writing, Mark introduced the concept of a rubric (NCTE 1998). "We're going to think of a few features of good fiction." The class brainstormed several features and, with Mark's guidance, they narrowed their list to:

1. character development
2. plot development
3. details
4. lead
5. mechanics

Next, for each feature of good writing, they created four characteristics, from very good to very weak, that they would use to evaluate their drafts. The class created these characteristics over a period of days, focusing on one feature per day, with some days for writing in between each day they spent on the development of their rubric.

They began with *character development*. Mark asked the class, "What are some characteristics of a poorly developed character?"

The students gave answers such as, "No description of the personality."

"No description of looks."

"The author is only telling you about the character, not showing you."

"No change occurs." During many book discussions, the class had talked about how characters change throughout a story. Often, the evolution of change in a character is the heart of a story.

Mark asked, "Would the reader care about this poorly developed character?"

"No," they answered.

Based on this discussion, Mark composed on the whiteboard this descriptor for a 1, a poorly developed character:

> No description of looks and/or personality, unrealistic character, only a few details and they tell about but don't show the character, nothing in character to care about, no change occurs.

Then Mark asked for the opposite: "What are some characteristics of a superbly developed character?"

The first student to answer said, "The writer shows the personality."

Another said, "The writer shows the looks."

"Would we have to write a four? It's the exact opposite of a one," one student observed. This student realized the criteria for a superbly developed character were the opposite of those they just had developed for a poorly developed one and thought maybe it wasn't necessary to continue with this discussion. Every class has a student who's one step ahead of everyone else.

Mark nodded, turned to the whiteboard, and created this descriptor for a 4, a superbly developed character:

Specific details that show clear personality and looks, realistic character development, reader gets to know and care about the character, a change occurs in the character.

They eventually created a total of four descriptors for each of the five elements of fiction and printed all of them on a huge chart. They referred to this rubric on the wall regularly and frequently. Students looked up at it while they worked, small groups referred to it when they met with Mark to confer about their drafts, and the students consulted it when someone read a draft to them and asked them to provide help with a certain feature. They also used it spontaneously when they told writers what they appreciated in their work and when they talked about the writing of professionals. They could use this rubric. They created it and understood it.

One day in a small group conference, Jessica wondered if the eight-year-old girl she had created for her character sounded like a child of that age, an age fourth graders think is somewhere in the ancient past. Her groupmates felt the character sounded like an eleven-year-old and they talked about the kinds of things they heard their younger siblings say. Eventually, Jessica wrote this to show the age of her young character:

> Mom and Jessica walked around the store. Mom wanted to hold her hand, but Jessica said, "Mom, I'm eight, I don't need to hold your hand anymore."

Mark's students learned to look carefully at their work and to more purposefully attend to all of its features. He said, "This rubric had the impact it did because of all the talk that went into it. We developed it together. Now my job is to keep referring to it, to have the kids look up at it, and look at it honestly. We constantly use it. We understand it so, so well.

"It's not only an evaluation tool, it's an instructional tool. In developing it, we referred to professional authors, such as Avi. We looked at the craft of writing and that's what helped us determine this continuum. Kids really recognize poor writing and quality writing. The rubric is almost like a third party that we are consulting. A rubric could be created for any area, science, whatever.

"The students can use this tool themselves. It really helps."

Mark used the distraction of the test to his students' ultimate advantage. Already committed to their writing, they wanted to put words together as effectively as possible and the addition of a rubric did not sap their energy.

Throughout the two years Mark devoted to this, he kept his focus on the high value he places on his students' engagement in their writing and reading. When his initial idea proved to be a distraction, he abandoned it. He and Ellen possess the convictions necessary to maintain the strong programs they have created, strengthen their programs with ideas that work, and not let intrusions lead them in unwarranted directions.

These teachers see themselves as learners. They purposely analyze their evaluation process and instructional plans all the time. In so doing, they try to understand each potential distraction for its problems and its merits. School days are tight, and they resolve to engage their students in valuable experiences.

Hmmmm . . .

Nancy Herdecker, as a fourth-grade teacher in Stratham, disciplined herself to make her own writing an integral part of her repertoire. She knew she wanted to write, and she knew this was significant to the teaching of writing (Bridges 1997). Sharing her own drafts with her class created anxiety. But her determination kept her self in line.

Nancy used her own writing to show various habits to her students. She taught them to respond to her and to respond similarly to one another. She wrote a one-page beginning of a draft about her two grandchildren and read it to her class. They loved the scene of the two children as one of them bounced balls off her garage door and the other tried unsuccessfully. Some of them had tried to bounce balls off their garages, also; some had succeeded and others had failed.

She read it again and asked them to listen for specific words and phrases they especially liked. This encouraged careful listening and gave Nancy helpful feedback. She liked knowing what was effective in her draft. She kept those gems.

Then Nancy read it a third time, preceded by a request, "As Nathan and Corina continued to play, Corina started to tease Nathan because he wasn't doing well. I want to hint at that future problem on this page, so please listen for spots where I might add something." She read.

They listened, and immediately four hands shot up.

After three suggestions, Nancy said thank you and closed the lesson with, "I'll work on this tonight and read it to you again tomorrow."

The next day, she shared her new first page, and her class heard that she took their suggestions seriously. Nancy asked, "What else would you like to know about what Corina and Nathan did?"

"Why didn't Nathan quit when she teased him?" one student asked.

"How did Corina learn to be so good?" another wondered.

Nancy answered their questions and promised to read them a further draft in a few days. Both she and they felt excited. The children were interested in her work.

Nancy asked them to think back to the four types of response they provided her, and they responded:

"We told you what we do."

"We gave you quotes."

"You asked for help and we did."

"We asked you questions."

Nancy explained how they would follow her pattern when they shared. This pattern became routine until they eventually moved away from it and conversed in a more natural fashion, all the while purposefully maintaining the same tone they would have used if they had been responding to Nancy. They understood the reason behind their practiced care. If someone uses words to slap a writer's fingers, the wounded writer may not feel like writing again.

Their self-discipline as responders ensured that, no matter their mood, they offered words of support. This made it possible for their classmates to keep their writing and reading alive.

Groups Eight

Karen Boettcher, a sixth-grade teacher in Manchester, wanted to get away from reading groups in which she peppered her students with comprehension questions, but what to do instead? Yes, somehow, they were to respond to the book rather than to her, but that was a vague guideline. One day when I observed her with a group that met to discuss *The Girl with the Silver Eyes*, by Willo Davis Roberts (1991), she opened the discussion with "Who'd like to start with a question to get the group moving?"

Ryan looked around at the others crowded around the table and asked a question that he proceeded to answer: "Do you like this book? It's interesting to find out how this girl uses her powers."

Artie immediately jumped in, then April, and forty exchanges of turns occurred, during which Karen took eleven turns. Kristin then made a comment about the girl's psychic powers, which brought a question from Karen: "What does that prove?"

Kristin replied, "She was just thinking of it and it happened."

Keisha elaborated, and eight more exchanges of conversation occurred among the students before Karen asked another question.

Later, when Karen and I met, she leaned forward and let her secret out of the bag: "Before the group today I told myself I wouldn't talk much. Too often I try to force my thoughts on them. I didn't read the chapters I assigned—on purpose. When I go around for conferences and they tell me about a book they have chosen to read that I haven't read, I can tell if they understand it."

And she could tell if these students understood this book. Karen trained herself to listen, to come to the group to find out what the students valued in it, and to take part in the discussions, as an informed reader. She *did* read the chapters on ensuing days.

In general, the talk pattern of traditional reading groups is that of an oral quiz. The teacher brings the students together to check their comprehension and proceeds to do so by asking them questions. Discussion to gain insights and to delight in the story isn't necessarily the order of the day; correct answers are.

Some educators study the talk patterns in groups. Teachers not only often govern the talk but typically talk differently to students whose achievement lags. They ask them questions to which the readers only need give short answers, rather than questions that require complicated thinking. And teachers ask students in low groups many questions about sounding out words, instead of also focusing on their personal connections to the information itself (Allington 1983).

At the present time in our profession, many educators question the age-old notion of bottom, middle, and top reading groups. The concerns arise from several sources, including scores that consistently and repeatedly show detrimental effects on students placed repeatedly in bottom groups. We can't place students in bottom groups in order to help them become better readers; it doesn't happen. Students in bottom groups regress.

For myself, in order to move away from the various negative aspects of bottom, middle, and top groups, I studied writing. In writing workshops, we don't divide writers into bottom, middle, and top writing groups. Thus, we have not developed different response patterns toward some writers, and we don't quiz students to find out if they comprehended a classmate's draft.

What do we do instead?

Groups Respond to Writing and Reading

When a small group of Linda Carey's students gathers to read their drafts to one another, they arrive with a myriad of compositions. Toward the end of September, one student in this multiage, grades 1–3 classroom brought a drawing of a football, another brought three pages of print about her weekend barbecue, a third brought a drawing and print about the class hamster, a fourth brought two pages of print about falcons, a fifth brought four pages of what was to become an alphabet book, and the sixth brought three illustrations that showed the story of *My Freedom Trip* (Park & Park 1998), a book Linda had read to the class.

Linda, who has a class of thirty, meets with six children each day, which means she meets with each child once a week in this type of writing group format. The child who composes her meanings via pictures learns from those who compose pages of print, and the children who have gained fluency with words learn about the intricacies of illustrations from their classmates. They all learn about one another's information and lives. Linda often brings a draft of her own writing to the group.

One day in this group little Licia told the others about her football: "I played football after school yesterday." Then Licia asked her groupmates, "What did you learn?"

The first to respond said, "I learned that you played football after school. Who did you play with?"

After this mini-conversation, another child said, "I learned that your football has writing on it."

After a mini-conversation in which they identified the brand of the football, Licia changed to the second question in the response format they were using at the time: "What does my writing remind you of?"

At this time, children told stories about the place of football in their lives, what they had done after school the day before, and the name brands of the clothes they were wearing.

During these workshops, each child takes a turn, asking for the two kinds of response, and Linda comes and goes. She stays with the group at times, in order to learn what the children are doing as writers-responders and to know what to teach them, but when she feels a strong pull from writers elsewhere in the classroom, she goes to them. Sometimes she leaves to move among the students in the classroom who are writing at their clusters of desks, often conversing as they work. She may conduct on-the-spot, brief writing conferences. She carefully teaches the children, via all-class mini-lessons, the procedures for groups and doesn't convene groups until the children can conduct them without her guidance. Of course, this doesn't mean they always run smoothly. Mini-lessons about small-group interactions continue throughout the year.

After morning recess, when this class has reading, six children again meet, but not in the same configurations as they use for writing groups each month. Linda, as with writing, convenes six children each day to read from books and talk about them. They each bring something they are now reading or learning to read. They bring books written by classmates, Linda, friends in other classrooms, children's magazines, and, of course, children's literature. Upon occasion, children bring cards and letters from home that they can read. And, once in a while, a child brings a clipping from a local newspaper, usually when someone known to the child makes news.

As each child takes a turn, they follow the same format they are currently using when they meet for writing groups. They read either the entire piece of writing they brought or a part of it and open the response with "What did you learn?"

One day, after the first volunteer read from *One Cow Coughs* (Loomis 1994), she asked, "What did you learn?"

Another child answered, "I learned to count backwards! Five, four, two, No! three. . . ." Several other children tried to count backward, and two other children told what they learned.

Then the child who read invited the second round of response: "What does my book remind you of?" They started talking about being sick and engaged in a lively discussion until it was another child's turn to read to them.

The second child read from *My Freedom Trip* (Park & Park 1998) and they responded similarly.

Throughout the year, in this classroom and other elementary classrooms, the children learn additional response patterns and gradually become adept at a large repertoire of comments, questions, and stories to tell. The teacher establishes some of the response formats when she hears the children use them in spontaneous talk: "Oh! That book reminds me of. . . ." At other times, she introduces response patterns that she thinks the children need in order to grow as writers-readers, such as one month when they focused a portion of their response on active verbs. Overall, they learn how to talk about what they read by using their talk about their own writing as a guideline.

Groups Change

Another feature of the age-old pattern for reading groups was the stationary nature of the groups. Teachers tended to keep students in groups throughout an entire school year and even for several consecutive years. Very seldom did children move from one group up—or down—to another. A child placed in the bottom group in first grade tended to remain there throughout his school years.

I was one of those teachers. When I started to teach I knew of no other way. I placed my students in bottom, middle, and top groups—sometimes I formed five groups!—and the great majority of them stayed in their groups for the year. Similarly, when I was a reading resource teacher, I went into classrooms to teach only the bottom group, and I taught some of those same children for three consecutive years. Very few moved higher. I shudder now, but it was the only teaching process I knew. I thought I was doing the best for each child. Thankfully, we now know how to teach without forming these unfortunate groups.

As with types of response patterns, I learned about nonpermanent groups when I studied writing instruction in many teachers' classrooms. The purpose of conferring with others about writing is to use the others as resources, and if writers share with only a small group for an entire year, the range of help available is narrow, so instead, groups change.

Sometimes writers feel comfortable with persons they know well, and it helps them to remain with a particular group for awhile, but not for more than a few weeks. Then, if a writer still feels unsure, some of the group members can change, and two or three who are steadfast supporters of the tentative writer can remain. Regardless, the group gains new blood, new thoughts.

The same holds true for adults. In my university classes, the teachers form groups to share their writing, reading, and teaching processes. They grow attached to the members of their groups and feel disoriented when I require them, after a few sessions, to form new groups. However, they soon learn that persons in these new groups notice and say things that no one in their original groups ever said. Their original, wonderful groups would have limited their learning.

Some of the teachers in my classes learn of the personal importance of small groups to their own growth. For many of them, the small group is the setting in which they speak most readily. We talk about this frequently, both in terms of our university class and in terms of the teachers' own students. The move away from small groups to sessions only for the entire class, which has happened in some localities, makes no sense for some students (Johnston 1997). The teachers in my, classes experience this firsthand.

They return to their classrooms with various ways to organize groups and change them to keep them fresh. One idea is to let the students decide, given parameters. The teacher gives the students three choices: change in four, six, or eight weeks. The class discusses and votes.

Another idea is for one student in the class to have the task of group formation as one of the weekly jobs. As this class helper walks around with the clipboard on which is a sheet with a workable number of lines per day, each student signs up to meet on a particular day to share in a group. Students can sign up in this way for writing, reading-writing, and/or reading groups, whichever is the format for the classroom.

In more than one classroom where I have served as a researcher, two configurations of reading groups coexisted. Each student met weekly with one group to which each member brought the book (or magazine or something else) of his own choice that he was reading and with another group, in which every member was reading the same book. When Karen Boettcher taught sixth grade, she organized these latter groups in the following way: When the class was ready to begin a new set of books, she sent five children to the bookroom, and each chose a title he wanted to read next. The class perused the five titles and each person signed up for a book of his choice. Each group decided upon the number of pages to read each week and created an approach to the discussions.

Karen taught various talk possibilities when she read to the class. In those settings, for example, she asked students to listen for vocabulary they weren't sure of, sections that tugged at their emotions, portions they found confusing, connections to their own lives, and various aspects of the craft of writing. One day when she read to them from *Out of the Dust*, by Karen Hesse (1997), they talked about the free-verse format as different from prose, a difficult technique, but one Mirabella decided to try in the memoir she was writing at the time.

Later, in her writing group, Mirabella again commented on her plans. During the same session, Samantha pointed out the word *strife* in the book she shared and said she intended to use it in a draft she was writing. Jonathan, a writer of books about various musical instruments, regularly showed them various ways to display nonfiction information.

Throughout the year, as the composition of the groups change, the students benefit from the various talents of the myriad of readers and writers in their classroom.

Groups Are Diverse Collections of People

Heterogeneous groups can confuse us. It sometimes seems impossible to conceptualize a group such as the one I mentioned earlier in which children in grades 1–3 all meet together. However, when we look at the wide span of interests and talents held by writers, and feel the vulnerability writers feel as they go public, we know they desperately need support from a wide span of fans.

Inexperienced writers learn more from experienced ones than they do from other inexperienced writers. When Ellen Blackburn Karelitz's classroom of first graders contained eight students who could not write their names, she scattered those children throughout the classroom. They wrote at tables with students who could write their names and, in a few cases, could write more than one sentence to form short narratives. Those eight children learned to write more quickly than if they had met every day with only one another, which is what Ellen would have had them do if she had believed in the principle of low groups.

Our profession, however, is laced with thoughts against heterogeneity. Not only do we segregate students into groups, we separate elementary, middle school, high school, and university teachers. As a university teacher, however, I have learned a great deal about teaching from my research in elementary and secondary classrooms. My own teaching has changed drastically; I base much of what I do as a university teacher on what I learn in the classrooms of elementary, middle, and high school teachers.

I didn't realize the importance of what I could learn from others until I had been a researcher for nine years. During those first years, each research project included a narrow range of teachers. Now, don't get me wrong, it was wonderful to initially learn about writing in one classroom, in two visits each week, for two years. I would choose that procedure again. Then, I moved into projects that spanned all grades in elementary schools, and those were excellent years.

But, when several of us created the project that spanned grades 1–12, my belief in heterogeneous groups intensified. For six years, several of us researched *students as evaluators* in Manchester, NH and collected data in several schools. All of us, both those of us from the University of New Hampshire and the classroom teachers, met twice each month to share our data. We wrote one-page research memos about what our data showed, about what the students did, and about what we were trying to do to teach the students to become increasingly adept as evaluators of themselves, one another, and their work. At our meetings, we distributed our one-pagers, read them to the group, and our colleagues supported our forays into new teaching territory, translated our specific techniques into general principles, and created similar techniques to try at their own grade levels.

But, all did not go well at first. When we adults first met, a strange chemistry dominated. The elementary and secondary teachers appeared to live in two different worlds and didn't seem to see the others' world as one from which they could gain ideas for their own teaching. The elementary teachers sort of held the high school teachers in awe—and they didn't even know them. Their awe represented an overall feeling of "you are above me." Similarly, it had evidently never occurred to the secondary teachers that they could grow as teachers by learning about the trials and errors of elementary children.

An underlying belief in the value of diversity did not exist, even though the ultimate goal of school is to support a more just and democratic society (Dudley-Marling 1997). Viewing a wide range of persons as a rich source of information to find value in did not drive our meetings. We needed to each figure out which stories from our classrooms would be perceived as valuable by the group. Eventually, this became less of a task as we became increasingly adept at finding ourselves in one another's data.

When Karen Harris Baroody's elementary special education students started to set goals for themselves as writers, Jody Coughlin, a junior high English teacher, decided that her students could probably do that. Over the course of time, it became common to hear someone say as we left a meeting, "Wasn't that the best meeting?"

In order to know exactly what was happening in these meetings, I recorded our discussions and analyzed our talk. I found a theme and several smaller patterns in our talk. Overall, we gave one another the nerve to push forward with something new and different amidst the more conservative approaches to education that persisted in that district and prevailed in our nation.

Specifically, we (1) consciously established connections among ourselves, (2) celebrated new ideas, (3) asked questions to move ourselves and one another forward, and (4) discussed problems.

Establishing Connections The connections we established among ourselves created the bedrock upon which we operated. We learned about the singing group one of us belonged to, the old home one of us renovated, and someone's blind father. We needed to know one another well so we could talk freely about the challenges in this project. The casual tone as we ate at the beginning of each after-school meeting helped us learn about our various weekend activities and families. We made no attempt to isolate our teaching from our out-of-school lives. It would have been an impossible task in a group of people who became so interested in one another's well-being—a prime lesson for our classrooms.

Upon occasion we shared the novels and other books we read for personal reading, and those conversations reinforced our interpersonal connections. We learned that some of our parents don't read, of Jane Kearns' devotion to Ireland, her ancestral homeland, and of Danling Fu's concerns for China, her birth country.

As fascinating individuals, we all had one thing in common. We were all new to the topic of our research: *students as evaluators.* When we wrote and shared our one-pagers, we learned of similar difficulties among us, such as how to introduce students to portfolios each year. Among us, we tried several strategies and borrowed from one another. Some of us invited a few students who had created portfolios in our classrooms the previous year to share those portfolios with our new classes. Some of us introduced portfolios by sharing our own, and others introduced them when students became immersed in their reading and writing and started to plan ahead. At that point, when they started to take off on their own, we knew they were readers and writers, and it would make sense for them to create portfolios to document their lives as such.

Celebrating New Ideas When Kathy Mirabile invited her students to find original documents and use them to create family histories, students became involved in U.S. history in ways her students had not throughout her entire career. As she continued to turn her classroom into one in which students found value in their schoolwork, we all considered that aspect of *students as evaluators* more seriously. We wanted the Manchester students to find value in their work.

New ideas about research techniques also spread. Jody Coughlin interviewed her students to find out what value they saw in the portfolios they had started to create, and she wrote about their answers in her one-pager. This was the first time any of us had collected interview data, as different from observational data, and for our next meeting, two other teachers collected this new kind of data. Others did so throughout the project.

Questioning Our Teaching When Jane Kearns read her one-pager about a male high school student who seldom participated in class, but who volunteered to be the first to share when they started to share portfolio entries, she raised a question fundamental to our project: *Why did this young man step forward?*

He was more excited than he had ever been in that class. When his teacher invited him to create a picture of himself, he found himself immersed in an assignment he wanted to do. He knew who he was: an artist. He shared several drawings; a certificate of achievement for his drawing; a copy of a check he had received for a promotional flier he had designed; a book by his guru, Charles Adams; a comic book in progress; an *Outland* comic strip; and a *Calvin and Hobbs* strip, about which he said, "Ingenious. Need I say more?" None of this was work from his English class. *Why not?*

We talked about the various students who appeared to be alienated and realized that many of them probably had interests they could pursue in English class (Saavedra 1999). In general, their teachers invited them to do so when they opened topic and genre choice, but students had employed some heretofore unknown to us criteria that narrowed their choices. Whereas the teachers had not intended to limit choices, they had led students to think that some of their most prized topics and genres would be unacceptable. The English teacher, for example, had not specifically offered the writing of cartoons as a possibility, so this young man had chosen topics and genres for his previous classwork that were, at best, lukewarm to him.

The portfolios started to bridge the chasm between life and school. The students finally believed that we were genuinely interested in who they were. They no longer had to sit and stare out the windows, planning their after-hours literacy endeavors. They could bring them into the classroom workshops, regardless of age. Grade 1 children could create cards to send to parents in prison, and when grade 4 children brought artifacts to show their after-school activities, they started to realize how often they took risks in those endeavors. They then started to purposefully maintain that personae as readers and writers in school. And, local newspapers will take articles about sixth graders' athletic events written by sixth-grade journalists. Choices in writing workshops expanded as we shared across grade levels.

Bringing Problems to the Group When we experienced problems, we brought them to the group. Sometimes the new ideas that evolved from our discussions about evaluation were not so easy to bring into being. Barbara, a high school English teacher, wrote about students who wouldn't put papers in their portfolios if she had placed a grade on them that they didn't like, a real issue for students who are to be evaluators. In her one-pager she wrote, "Sometimes my focus needs to switch from the writing to the writer's faltering confidence in order to insure that she will be strong enough to take chances in her writing . . . . WHAT to see—the writer or the writing?"

We pondered this. Is there a difference? Maybe it's not a matter of switching focus. Maybe to focus on a writer's faltering confidence is to focus on her writing; if her confidence is shot, what hope does she have for herself as a writer? The question of whether to see the writer or the writing became "Is it possible to separate the two?"

As we talked, Bill Wansart said, "Why should they take a chance and write something personal if they might get a C on it? When you share your own writing with them, they talk, but when they share their writing with you, you not only talk, you grade it." Sometimes students write in personally strong voices, but a C might squelch that strong voice and it might not appear again, sometimes for years. This is serious. Writers must feel strength in the voices; the voice of a writer is her hallmark. All writers sound different from one another. In all of our meetings, we never resolved the grading issue, but we did learn that if we are to grade individual papers, we must write those evaluations on separate sheets of paper. We must not violate the students' work.

We also learned that the students need to evaluate their work before we do. Not only do their evaluations inform us, but the students learn to take an appreciative, critical look at their drafts. Their ability to evaluate their own work is what will get them through life; they can not rely on a teacher. Just as discipline must be internal, so must evaluation.

It is this internal sense of our own value that the diversity within our group awarded to each of us. This enlarged sense of our own worth allowed us to say, "Hmmm. You're doing something I've never done. I think I'll adapt it and try it. What would you think if. . . ?" The elementary teachers no longer viewed the secondary teachers as too far above them to learn from, and the secondary teachers had learned to use their elementary friends' ideas in their own classrooms.

What a splendid difference diversity can make.

Hmmmm . . .

Four sixth-grade boys meet as a writing group, two of them determined to weave their current, awesome moves into fiction about themselves as professional ballplayers. Of the two athletes, one loves baseball and the other basketball. Determined to become professionals, they study players' moves when they attend games, watch TV, and rent movies. They play and practice with diligence. These boys read sports magazines, articles, and books. Each has started to write a newspaper story dated 2011 about himself as a star in a professional game.

These boys and some of their classmates, at an earlier point in the year, could have cared less about writing. It was a bore. Sharmane, their teacher, challenged them to think of their writing in new ways. The class generated lists of possible types of writing they had not tried, and she urged them to find a genre into which their passions fit.

To take up their teacher's challenge, these two athletes met with two friends and the four of them brainstormed ways of writing they had not used but could use as present and future athletes. With various forms of reading spread before them, and ideas flying, they came up with the idea to write these 2011 news clippings. "Hey! I could write a scrapbookful!"

They studied the language of sports writers in more than one newspaper and, in effect, these two boys are changing their sparse personal narratives into fiction in which they are pros. As they meet on this day they envision incredible moves, a challenge they welcome, and their group helps them fantasize these hypothetical games. Their voices sound animated, a tone Sharmane has sought—the excited conversation of a group involved in its work.

Across the Curriculum | Nine

When I met with Karen Boettcher in August prior to my entry into her classroom as a researcher, I said, "So, our plan is for me to take notes on what happens when your students evaluate themselves as readers and writers. When do you suggest I come?" Karens said, "We read and write all day long."

I shifted gears fast. I had planned to spend a few hours in Karen's classroom each time I went, but instead I went to her sixth grade twice a week for two years and stayed for the entire day. Karen's students wrote in science and read interesting materials in social studies, but my prior interest in the language arts prevailed. I didn't become as engaged in the content areas as I now wish I had. Unfortunately, I focused on the language arts. I wore blinders. In this way I represent many who have researched reading and writing over the years. We have collected much more data on reading and writing as it's done during the language arts period than throughout the day, and some educators criticize us.

Our apparent focus on personal narratives as the dominant genre within research on writing instruction leaves teachers out on a limb in their search for ways to incorporate writing instruction across the day. Writers in many domains, however, share commonalties, regardless of whether they are poets, mathematicians, or scientists. Our goal is for our students to become thoughtfully, purposefully, and excitedly immersed in learning. As literacy teachers, we believe in writing, reading, art, talking, and listening as useful processes for students to use as learners. We don't care what kind of writing or reading sweeps them into the world of learning. We work and work to help them find topics that engulf them.

Some of our students find their entry point in music class when they write songs about their complicated lives, others could write personal narratives about their friends for months on end, and some are more fascinated by science than anything else. Many use the Internet and pursue topics they could not study otherwise, such as one preservice teacher in a content-area reading class who learned about extinct Australian marsupials.

Three principles underlie instruction and evaluation across the curriculum, regardless of whether the scene surrounds a sixth grader who is writing about grasshoppers or a second-grade child who is learning about his own birthday party. In this chapter I will elaborate on each in sections about science, social studies, and math:

1. Writers, readers, and evaluators write, read, and evaluate as ways to learn about something.
2. Writers, readers, and evaluators consider various ways to acquire, organize, and present information.
3. Writers, readers, and evaluators—both students and teachers—become energized by their work.

Science

The process of writing her column usually helps a columnist figure out what she learned when she interviewed a local environmentalist. When this writer initially sits down to write, her notes are a jumble, but as she plans and writes, she ferrets out the focus of her article. Or, maybe, much to her relief, it became clear during the interview and she writes it, presto, in a first draft. Regardless, she figures out her focus while in the midst of her task. She can't do so before she interviews the environmentalist because she remains open to what she will learn in the interview.

1. Writers, readers, and evaluators write, read, and evaluate as ways to learn about something.

This is one of the most important features of writers, which we have acquired from professionals.

Often, writers figure out what they want to say while they are in the process of writing. The process of writing includes the data collection phase and everything else the writer does to accomplish a particular writing act. This stance—that writers write to learn—is contrary to the stance taken a few decades ago, when it was more common to use writing as a way for students to show what they knew. A basic dilemma over whether writers know something and then write it down or use the process of writing as a learning tool (in the same way we read to learn and listen to learn) influences what writing experiences teachers create for their students. Whereas shades of both positions rightfully demand recognition, our profession's shift away from the former stance represents a huge change.

Consider the sixth-grade girl who caught a grasshopper, used a magnifying glass to study him for three days in a jar, gathered information about him, and then asked questions as she wrote her lab report, such as "What is more important? What do I omit?"

When Isabella evaluated her draft as she prepared for her turn during share time, she decided to ask for advice: "I learned about how he moves and sees, but I learned most about what he eats, and I decided to just write and draw about his eating. Is that OK, or should I tell about everything?" Other students gave different opinions, but one comment stood out: "I think it's gross how you drew food hanging from his mouth!" This comment and a few questions about eating confirmed for Isabella that it was OK to focus on her grasshopper's eating habits. Someone asked, "How often does he eat?" and "What about when grasshoppers attack in flocks and eat acres?" Isabella didn't know but found these questions interesting. She went off to seek more information.

2. Writers, readers, and evaluators consider various ways to acquire, organize, and present information.

Science materials come in all shapes, sizes, and formats. Students study various presentation styles and consider options as they try to figure out what will be the most effective way to present their important information.

Isabella considered three ways to incorporate her information about her grasshopper's mouth parts into her writing. "I could create a glossary for the end of my article, or I could write about each mouth part in a paragraph, or I could create sort of a graph." She decided on an option and later explained, "I decided to put the mouth parts into a box over on the side. I saw that in one of the books about grasshoppers, and I wanted to learn how to create an insert on the computer. And, I finally figured it out!"

While these students write, whether in science or in other classes, their teachers move among them, and as they do, they glean ideas for what to teach. After Isabella shared her box-making process, Karen Boettcher, over a few days, taught options for ways to insert vocabulary explanations into their writing. On one day, Isabella taught her "box technique" and provided follow-up help to students who chose to use it.

Providing lessons that students see as timely for their current writing has proven to be one of the greatest challenges of recent decades of writing instruction. Of all the various skills and strategies the students in a class need on any given day, it can often be overwhelming for a teacher to decide which one(s) to teach. Karen addresses many needs on the spot as she moves around the room; some she delegates to other children, and a few she chooses to turn into lessons for groups or the class. In Isabella's class, she could have taught a lesson on various ways to close a piece of informational writing of this type, which was a concern of more than one child, but many students seemed to be sharing ideas for closings on their own. Thus, she chose to focus a series of lessons on ways to incorporate vocabulary.

Teachers make decisions about their teaching—and writing— processes, students about their writing—and teaching—processes, and they all talk about the various options they consider.

3. Writers, readers, and evaluators—both students and teachers— become energized by their work.

I know it sounds idealistic to present a class as if all the students feel excited about their writing, but a goal of self-evaluation is for students to become and remain enthused. With the support of all, each student figures out what to study and how to go about it in an interesting way. Energetic learners get further than bored ones; they value their work.

Isabella's friends' interest in her grasshopper fed into her emerging interest. They had their own specimens, but during science workshop they commented on the creature in her jar, just as she commented on theirs. Their genuine curiosity about one another's endeavors kept their energy up.

Some teachers foster this energy by not drawing lines during the day. When it's time for writing workshop, students can choose to devote their time to whichever writing project they choose. Some of them work on personal narratives and others, their science explorations. Writing is writing, and it can be confusing if the writing for language arts is labeled *writing*, and the writing for science is labeled *science*. A way to streamline time and teach various subjects from one philosophical perspective is to merge efforts when possible.

For one of our Manchester research group meetings, Jim Pottle wrote about his student teacher's pumpkin unit:

> On Monday the class discussed their pumpkin unit from the previous week. My student teacher led them as they charted all the experiences and then they identified what skills they had used to complete the tasks. In the end, they had a huge web on the blackboard that connected all the subject areas. The students were amazed that they had studied all the subject areas without one textbook assignment. Then they asked, "Did you plan it that way?" One student remarked, "That's a sneaky way to get us to learn."

Maybe so; it's also efficient and wise.

Students often have more than one writing project going; we have given concurrent assignments in various subjects for years. Typically, however, we kept the various subjects separate. Work on your science now; work on your language arts next hour. Nowadays, however, some teachers merge various subjects. When it's time for writing, it's time for writing. Students work on their science or their language arts, as long as they keep deadlines in mind. Juggling their time is a life skill that requires much practice. When these students meet in small groups or as a class to share their drafts for response, the various kinds of writing appear back to back. The demands of various writing tasks overlap and differ. Studying various forms in one sitting can help writers see writing as a helpful process of learning that they can use in many settings.

Social Studies

The variety of writing students do in social studies is vast, and the same three principles underlie instruction as in science.

1. Writers, readers, and evaluators write, read, and evaluate as ways to learn about something.

When Jan Roberts' third graders studied Colonial New England they went to York, Maine, to spend a day in a living history museum of several restored buildings. Each child took notes during the trip and later chose an aspect of the trip to think about further via writing. Chad wrote about the bus ride in "On the Way to York, Maine"; Sarah wrote about the old schoolhouse; Brent wrote about the gundalow boat; and Justin wove his thoughts about the arrival of the first European ship into this poem:

Ship Ahoy

The ship is coming in! All of the townspeople
were gathered around the John Hancock Wharf and
warehouse to see the first European ship come in.
Ho, the ship is coming in.
I'm sure. I don't have the
slightest doubt it isn't docking here!
I'll be ashamed of everyone
if it doesn't come in.
Oh, the ship is coming in!

When Justin shared his final draft with the class, he sang the last line to the tune of "Glory, Glory Alleluia," much to his classmates' enjoyment.

Overall, these third graders talked, read, experienced, evaluated, read, and wrote to learn. They read about the colonists, shared the information they each gained, and experienced the lives of colonists at the living history museum. They wrote throughout the day, studied their notes to find particular areas of interest, and wrote some more. Some of them searched for additional information, some revised, and all published their work in a collection for the school library to be used by the next year's students and any other interested persons.

2. Writers, readers, and evaluators consider various ways to acquire, organize, and present information.

When they returned from their trip they held an evaluative session about what they had learned and why. Sarah had learned a great deal about students' lives when the Colonial teacher immersed them in a lesson. "The drama helped me learn. I know that for sure!" she said. Others had appreciated the question-answer format arranged by some of the colonists. A few mentioned information they remembered from the pre-tour movie. This discussion helped them think of various ways information can be acquired and organized.

As they became involved in additional reading, some students became fascinated by the author's note that occasionally appears at the end of a piece of historical fiction and considered writing some as part of the books they might create. They discussed whether, as readers, they preferred to read the note before they read the book or after, again noting differences among them.

As they wrote about Colonial times, they talked about their writing processes along the way. Sarah had never before written, researched, written, and researched again as she did while she learned about hornbooks. She collected, selected, collected, and selected as she wrote. All of the children served as teachers, with Jan as their overall instructor. Justin appreciated her suggestion to turn his information into a poem, and Sarah appreciated Melinda's comment: "Why don't you phone the museum teacher? I bet she'll tell you something neat about hornbooks. Maybe you could write your whole piece like a conversation."

3. Writers, readers, and evaluators—both students and teachers—become energized by their work.

It's relatively easy to generate enthusiasm before a trip and to maintain the interest during the excursion, but upon reentry to the classroom, the challenge to keep the energy high becomes real. The focus on what each student finds interesting helps. So do the decisions they each make as writers when they create their own formats, from poetry, to historical fiction, to letters, to a story for an early reading book, to nonfiction essays.

The diversity helps keep the energy high. Most students appreciate the challenge of creating something of their own. They like surprises, such as the music of Justin's last line.

A different angle on writing in social studies comes from an approach Mark Milliken used for awhile when he taught fifth grade in Stratham. His students wrote responses to, not summaries of, the sections they read from their social studies text. One day a girl wrote:

> I didn't like the section on Pizarro. He was an evil man the way he plundered the villages and killed the people who lived there, but the author of the text didn't even say he shouldn't have acted that way. It even made him sound like a hero. I got really mad.

The students used these written responses as the basis of their discussions, which brought them to look afresh at what they read. To them, not only did history become a lesson in what was, but it also led them to dream of what could be. The students became articulate about their world and themselves. This girl's reflection opened the day's discussion, and, in general, from that day on, these fifth graders kept their critical thinking skills in high gear.

Math

I didn't mention writing in math in my original version of this book. However, I recently studied writing in math with six K–5 elementary teachers and other University of New Hampshire personnel. I visited elementary classrooms twice a month for two and a half years and learned a great deal. When I was an elementary teacher, I taught math, but now I have gained a deeper understanding of its relationship to literacy. When they write and read in various ways during math class, these teachers and children do much more than compute right answers to problems posed in workbooks.

In the first- and second-grade multiage classroom of Debbie Nichols in Rollinsford, a very small town in New Hampshire, the children write across the day, which is very important in primary classrooms. Content-related writing is connected to young children's growth as readers (Dickinson & DiGisi 1998), and Debbie's children have many opportunities to write. During math, their first subject each morning, their work exemplifies the three principles of learning.

1. Writers, readers, and evaluators write, read, and evaluate as ways to learn about something.

Each year Debbie tries different ways for her young children to learn about their community. For example, the children may design Kids' Town, a transformation of their classroom into a community in which they study math, writing, and reading. For several weeks they operate a pizza parlor, a library, a craft shop, a pet store, and a post office.

In the post office they buy paper, envelopes, and stamps. Then they write to classmates, mail their letters by placing them in classmates' mailboxes, and read them with excitement. One day when business at the post office boomed, one of the post office workers created this sign: FOORM LIN HEER. Many forms of writing, math, and evaluation exist in this "real" town.

The children who run the stores each day keep track of their income and expenses. One class created a system of credit cards after they learned that their parents receive bills for their use of them. The students had thought credit cards were free! Each store has its own account at the bank.

In the Town Library, a child takes on the role of librarian and reads to children. Depending on the teacherly bent of the child, we may see behaviors similar to those I encourage in my teacher education classes. Sometimes I read literature that is obviously related to math (Schiro 1997), but often I read regular children's literature and ask the audience to be on the alert for embedded math. For example, *Only Opal*, by Barbara Cooney (1994), is the autobiographical account of a young girl who was an orphan in the early years of this century and is not written with math in mind, but when I read it to a group, they found several mathematics concepts. They noticed the shadows, a dozen eggs, and weekly events. When teachers frequently invite students to look for math in books, they start to do this on their own.

In one teacher's class, when Monette read *Yunmi and Halmoni's Trip*, by Sook Nyul Choi (1997), she immediately started to talk about the semicircle shape of the mandoo dumplings. In the story, the girls created "half-moons," and the comparison strengthened Monette's understanding of geometry. She began to look routinely for math in the books she read, and she and her classmates began to see math on their refrigerators and in their sidewalk games. They knew that when the class stood in order from shortest to tallest for a photo, they were engaged in math.

2. Writers, readers, and evaluators consider various ways to acquire, organize, and present information.

Debbie is on the alert for mathematical moments and builds time for reflection about them into the hectic school day. She and her children often talk about various ways to pursue a problem. One day as they gathered at the end of their enactment of Kids' Town, a child began, "I gave Yvette the correct change for a thirty-three-cent stamp when she gave me a dollar!"

"Yvette, what did the postmistress give you?" Debbie asked.

Not without some pauses, Yvette said, "Two quarters, three nickels, and two pennies."

The class clapped.

Then, Debbie said, "Let's think of two other ways the post-mistress could have created the correct change." She is constantly on the vigil against one correct answer and encourages the children to create options whenever possible (Trafton & Hartman 1997). They have many conversations about the various ways individual children think through situations (Whitin & Whitin 2000).

3. Writers, readers, and evaluators—both students and teachers—become energized by their work.

The intent of response is to energize students, and Debbie works very hard to keep the children from becoming discouraged. She creates an overall climate in which they think nothing of saying, "I need help!" During an enactment of Kids' Town, I heard children ask others, "What should I charge for this?" "Can I buy two stamps with this much money?" "Which pet eats more expensive food?"

When the class meets to discuss Kids' Town, children offer concerns as readily as successes. Some of them don't have enough business, some think their friends buy too much junk food, and some want help to fold paper into envelopes. Response brings about teaching and a class that seeks it is a collection of learners.

Tim O'Keefe (Mills, O'Keefe, & Whitin 1996) wrote about the day helium balloons intrigued his primary students and diverted him from his planned lesson on estimation. When the class went on a field trip to a supermarket, the florist gave every child a balloon and the children, upon returning to their classroom, tied them to the backs of their chairs. Regular school became more and more difficult. Eventually, one girl captured Tim's attention when she said, "I wonder what my balloon will pick up" (188).

Tim asked, "What do you mean?"

"What sorts of things would my balloon hold up if I tied them on?"

"How could you find out?"

The children experimented and created charts, as they had done with other kinds of information on previous occasions. To publish a chart or graph is to author mathematical information. To walk around with a clipboard to collect data is to behave as a researcher, mathematician, scientist, reader, learner, and writer. Of the many tasks of writers, one is to gather information, and this is one way to do so. Of the many formats writers use to publish their information, charts are one.

Tim and his students also kept a classroom math journal. Anyone could write in it at any time and all, including Tim, did. When new entries appeared, Tim set aside time for the person to share the new entry—another type of writing and another opportunity for a learner to make learning relevant to his life.

Hmmmm . . .

Debbie Nichols jumped for joy when she found math in the child's daily journal entry (shown in Figure 9-1). Debbie's students had been writing in math in as many ways as Debbie could think of, from signs to story problems (Brown 1997), but until then no one had spontaneously used math in any of his or her own writing.

Writing across the curriculum enlarges students' worlds. They see details they might otherwise not notice, become skilled at writing techniques they may otherwise never use, and learn to appreciate well-written nonfiction magazines and books (Harvey 1998). Evaluation across the curriculum—the process of finding value in the various curricular areas—opens reading-writing doors for many students who love the information of the various sciences.

Students become sensitive to areas of interest throughout the day and start to turn to curriculum topics when they choose their own topics for writing and reading. Reading and writing become ways to explore their fascinating world.

> Today is my sisters half Birthday. She is nine and a half agsakly And tommorow is my Dad half Birthday. But to be agSackt my SistersHalfBirthday is from noon to noon yestertday from twelwr o'clock at lunch to twelwvoclock today that is my sisters rell half Birthday unlus there is a leeper because you can not split 365 Days in half Because it iso odd number But if it has aeleper it will have one moreDay and it will be an even numbes so you can cut itin half.

Figure 9-1. Math in a journal entry.

Across the Grades | Ten

When writers of all ages read, whether they be in the primary grades or older, they look for something they can use. Writers regularly look to other writers for big ideas, clever vocabulary words, and helpful strategies.

When I read "When Life Begins!," one of the stories in J. California Cooper's collection *Homemade Love* (1996), her overt organizational strategy intrigued me:

> This story is shaped like a Y. Two paths lead to one road. I got to tell you two things, or stories, before I get to the main road where it all comes together!

Then, after the first "thing, or story," she reminded me of her plan:

> Now, we got to go back and start at the other side of that Y and come down to the part where the paths meet and join.

Finally, after the second story, she wrote:

> Now! We at the fork of the Y where the two paths join into one road of life!

As a writer who reads, I am in the midst of a draft about one of my grandmothers, and I can't seem to figure out an effective organization for it. I don't know if I'll use this Y strategy, but maybe I'll make my organizational strategy overt. I think it's sort of a straightforward way to probably resolve my dilemma, and

I'm sort of a straightforward person, so it may be a strategy that will work for me.

Young writers think of their writing while they read, too. When eight-year-old Jennifer was nearly finished with a piece of nonfiction about sponges, she kept thinking, "What will I write next? I could write about another warm-water sea creature. I think they're my passion, but I sort of want to write something different and come back to ocean life later. I could write about winter. That would be way different and fun. I've had some scary snow times." As she perused the bookshelves, she noticed *Snowflake Bentley* (Martin 1998), illustrated by Mary Azarian, and read it instantly from cover to cover. Mary Azarian's award-winning skill with woodcuts prompted Jenn to experiment with prints as a form of artwork, and she decided to write a book about Mary Azarian.

Finding ideas in the work of other writers is one of the many processes used by writers of all age levels. In some ways, the teaching of writing varies little from grade to grade. In this chapter I feature some of the commonalties among writers that lead to similar instruction by teachers of both the young and not-so-young: the use of artwork, the use of invented spellings, and the use of workshops.

Artwork

Many writers of all ages draw. Some don't, but whether they do or don't is often unrelated to their age. Those who draw find it not only a useful part of their writing process but frequently a necessary part. Some draw before they write, others after, and others draw off and on while they write. They draw to help them figure out what something looks like, to help them think through a tough spot in their writing, and for relief.

For some of us, illustrations take the form of photos and slides. When I travel through a classroom with a lens before my eye, I zoom in to see students I may have overlooked, distance myself from others, and ignore some. I know I will show these slides to teachers elsewhere, and as I scan the classroom, I say to myself, "What's going on here? What's significant? What's irrelevant?"

One day while perusing Diane Conway's first-grade classroom, camera in hand, I noticed one little boy who was particularly intent. He held before him a book, and his juice-stained face was oh-so-serious. His fingers, certainly smudging this book, held it firmly. I zoomed in, snapped him, and then conferred with him. Jared proudly read a few pages, and I eventually asked, "How did you learn to read this?"

He rose and started to walk away! "I'll be right back," he said. Jared returned with his portfolio and opened to a two-part entry: his self-chosen artifact was a photocopy of the cover of the book, and he had written a reflection (an explanation of why he placed this artifact in his portfolio as evidence of his growth) in three of the margins of the photocopy:

> I LRNd to Read This Book
> I hav a nuTh Book at hom
> [I learned to read this book.
> I have another book at home.]

As we conversed, I learned that Jared had a second copy of this book at home and had practiced it both there and in school until he could read the entire book without help. Now he was practicing for fluency, and as soon as I walked away, he instantly became reengrossed in his self-assigned task.

My camera helps me find significant events and gives me opportunities to learn about them in the same way that a pencil, crayons, Play-Doh, paints, markers, music, and dance (Blecher & Jaffee 1998) do for other artists. Ansley Dauenhauer (1996) wrote about Sam, a boy in her third-grade class who initially didn't write, but when he began to value his artistic side, he could write. Similarly, but with wood, Margaret Voss (1996) conducted a case study of a fourth-grade boy whose woodworking skills showed her where his literacy skills lay.

Last spring in a reading course I taught, after we experimented with crayons, one teacher who works as a full-time aide for an upper-elementary student with multiple difficulties brought crayons for her student to use, if the student desired. These crayons appealed to the girl in a mild way, but she requested watercolors. Now the aide travels with a tray of watercolors. Whenever the girl wants throughout the day, she can use the watercolors to think, experiment, and get herself through a situation, academic or personal—the two mesh for her. She has become a new person.

Invented Spellings

Writers of all ages invent spellings. The idea of invented spelling comes to us from professional writers. They refuse to interrupt themselves when they are on a roll. Writers become involved in their work and don't want to break a line of thought with something as mundane as the spelling of a word. They just get it down and move forward. They don't want to break their momentum.

It was our profession's study of writers and our discovery of invented spelling as an important part of their writing processes that led us to realize one of the most important notions of the last several years. Very young children can write! As long as they know a few letter-sound correspondences, they can put themselves on paper. They can make their mark on the world, a liberating thrill.

Nowadays, writers of all ages go back and check their work with their spell checkers. Those who don't have access to computers refer to word lists, friends, editors, dictionaries, or various other resources, but the very young don't go back and correct their spellings. They can't; they don't have the skills to do so. They write for the sake of writing and continue to write one new piece of writing after another. They constantly move forward. Gradually, as they learn more letters and sounds taught to them by various people, they invent fewer spellings, and their inventions become less inventive.

The liberty to invent spellings not only makes it possible for little children to write, it makes it possible for writers of all ages to maintain their voices, their originality. They can use any word they want in their drafts. Spelling can't hold them back. Thus, children can write about what they value. David can write about the fire truck, Michael about Power Rangers (paeraJs), and Alyssa about her hamster (*hemstar. Is Nane Is Hershey. he Is Softe and quiet.*).

Deciding when to nudge children into more regular use of conventional spelling is always a dilemma. Children move from an understanding of single letters to clusters of letters and then into an understanding of how words work. They figure out the role of affixes and the derivations of words. We look at what students can do and at what is confusing to them; this is often one and the same. Alyssa, who wrote about her hamster, knows about the silent *e* in *name* but is confused about it in *softe*. She knows about the word *is* but confuses it with *his*. What to teach her?

A larger picture of her as a writer may be necessary, but given what we know, she could maybe sort out *is* and *his*. Maybe her use of *is* for *his* was a slip, or maybe she needs to listen for the /h/, which she can hear in *hamster*. I'd check out this possible confusion with the initial consonant sound of *h* before I would step into the silent *e* territory with this young child. The /h/ sound is not necessarily obvious, but this concept is more straightforward than the silent *e* principle.

Opportunities to invent spellings give young children much practice in phonics whenever they write. They sound out words all the time! And their teachers gain much information about what the children know and appear to be ready to learn, but the teaching of spelling remains problematic.

Kelly Chandler and the teachers in the Mapleton Teacher-Research Group (1999) in Maine studied spelling for a year. Among other self-generated tasks, they surveyed parents and learned of the difference between the parents' beliefs in spelling and those of the teachers. To 90 percent of the parents, perfection in spelling counts at all times. In contrast, to the teachers, spelling is, in part, an integral part of the exploration required of writers who draft. As part of their strategies to deal with this concern, the teachers decided to stop saying to their students, "Don't worry about spelling. It doesn't matter yet" (88). Instead, they resolved to use phrases like "Spell the best you can right now, and we'll work on making it better if this becomes a piece of writing you edit for publication."

Workshops

In classrooms, the *workshop* is often the place in which the writers and readers work. As with everything else in the teaching of writing and reading, workshops vary (Roller 1996), but over the years I have come to picture workshops as times during which five settings enable the workers to grow as writers, evaluators, and readers. I see these occurring in any order on most days, but some don't occur at all in the classrooms of excellent teachers:

- everyone works alone
- some workers interact
- the class gathers for Author's Chair sessions
- small groups meet to confer about their work
- workers celebrate their stretches in mini-lessons

Everyone Works Alone   Everyone includes the adults. Everyone works on his writing, reading, and evaluation tasks by himself. Students table any questions, comments, concerns, or joys until later. They all have lots to do, so a problem in one area can be ignored. The worker can work on a different piece of writing, read something else, or work on a portfolio entry. No one needs help with any task right now. The important thing during this time is to respect everyone's time to work.

In one class, a student had chosen to learn about soccer for a piece of writing of her choice and was reading an article about the previous night's game from the sports section of the local newspaper. Someone else was working on his assignment for the class unit on Thomas Jefferson by finding information about Jefferson on the Internet. Someone else was writing about a personal experience in the form of free-verse poetry, and a fourth student, who had just written a memoir, was arranging photos among portions of text. A fifth student was writing to his father, who lived out of state, and three girls were writing reflections about math for their portfolios. Writers typically work on more than one piece of writing at a time; readers often read more than one kind of writing in a day. Literate people busy themselves with many kinds of literacy.

In some kindergarten and first-grade classrooms in which I have studied writers who read, the teachers didn't set aside a work time during which everyone worked alone, and their decision makes sense to me. Some young children can't seem to read or write alone. They chatter with their friends at their tables while they write and they want to be with someone else when they read. It doesn't seem productive for them to work alone.

However, some teachers of these very young children do set aside a time when each person learns to work entirely alone. The quietness brings a serious atmosphere of work into the classroom, and the teachers appreciate the tone this creates. Working by oneself is a skill children can hone from their very early days in school.

Historically, our profession did not necessarily set aside time in school during which students—much less teachers—wrote and read. Teachers typically assigned writing as homework. The actual writing of a paper was not usually done during class time amidst other writers. It has taken us years to realize that the most important act of a writer is to write, and setting aside time in school for it is paramount. We value writing, and to show our value system, we set aside time for the classroom of writers—including ourselves—to write. We honor this act.

Reading seems to be even harder to value. Setting aside time in school for readers to read from materials of their choice is even less common, in my experience, than setting aside time for writers to work on their self-designed tasks. Actually, the two go together. Because we know about the importance of reading to writers, when we set aside time for writers to work, we know they will read as well as write.

Some teachers set aside this piece of time for students to work alone every day, some less often, and others set aside more than one work time throughout a day, but all ensure frequency and regularity. When a work time ends, the students know on what day and at what time and for how long their next work time will be. They need to plan ahead. Writers and readers are planners. Their tasks are hard, and in order to do them well they think about possibilities during luscious idle moments.

The amount of time teachers set aside for this work time varies from a few minutes to forty-five. More than one teacher in Stratham sets aside a block of forty-five minutes. That is a lot of time, and the writers and readers can get so involved they don't want to stop. The momentum builds.

Some Workers Interact   In my own classes, I signal the end of the alone work time by starting a conference with someone. As soon as I start to talk, my students know they may do likewise. Some have questions to ask others, and some have books or ideas to share. Some want to read their drafts to someone or to a couple of friends. They confer. Others continue to work on their own. The busyness of the workshop mounts during this time of interaction.

Teacher-student conferences during this time are both wonderful and problematic. They are wonderful, because it is so special to sit alone with a writer and learn her work. I love to hear about her life experiences, her teaching, and other information she has chosen to study, such as "Which guitar should I buy?" I find out what is going well and whether this writer has concerns.

If a writer wants a suggestion, I try not to give one. It is my goal that the two of us will generate at least two options so the writer leaves the conference with a decision to make, and I don't want the decision to be "Should I use Jane's suggestion or not?" I want the writer to have two or three—not six or eight—options from which to choose.

When I conferred with Bernadette about which guitar she should buy, I learned quite a bit about guitars. At least I could talk with her; my husband has three. Then she said, "I don't know how to organize this. I could list the various guitars and their plusses and minuses, or I could do something more interesting. What do you think?"

I wondered. Then I said, "Well, you could jazz up the list with illustrations of each guitar, or. . . ."

Bernadette interrupted, "I never think of illustrations. There are great ones in some of the promo lit. I could maybe do that."

"Or, maybe you could write it in the form of a conversation between a salesperson and you."

"Well, that might work. It could be a riot to create words for a pushy sales clerk! Or, I could have an e-mail conversation with this friend who knows lots about guitars."

"Great! You have ideas to think about." That's it! I walked away. Bernadette started to generate ideas and could move beyond where she was when we started to confer.

But it takes me all semester to have one conference with each student. At least that's better than none. The teachers in my classes do appreciate a few minutes with me alone.

The teachers in whose classrooms I have worked as a researcher create every imaginable schedule for individual conferences. Probably the most common is simply a class list, and the teacher confers with a small number every day, checks off each name, and eventually starts over. He records the conference instantly, such as I did after mine with Bernadette, before he moves to another student. These records provide such important information about each writer and provide information for teaching.

Many of the mini-lessons in my own classes are about transferring from our university classroom to the teachers' classrooms. The teachers share the words of our conferences and compare them to conferences they hold with their own students. Theirs are almost identical to the ones I conduct with them, regardless of whether their students are in grades 1, 4, or 6. These teachers learn from their students about music lessons, Beethoven, and new little puppies, just as I learned about guitars from Bernadette. And, similarly, they sometimes brainstorm the order in which to present information and illustrations. Children love to lay out pages in ways that effectively highlight their information.

We also talk about how conferences with me are similar to or different from the conferences they hold with their peers. These conferences they hold among themselves save the day. The teachers can't all turn to me whenever they have a question. What a logjam that would be.

Peer conferences are also a lifesaver for elementary classrooms. When students sit in clusters of desks or at tables with others who have expertises different from their own, they can easily chat while they work. Very important mini-lessons are those in which the students share the kinds of questions they ask one another, whom they ask, and what kinds of help they receive. A very important lesson for teachers is to not let students convince them they need them! Students very seldom need the teacher. Almost always, another student in the class can answer the question a student has. When students know one another well and know how to respond to requests—another mini-lesson topic—the interaction time works.

During this time, many students do accomplish a great deal. They know it is their responsibility to get up and go for help if they need it. The unavailability of human resources cannot stand in the way of their forward motion. People surround the writers, and they turn to them.

Entire Class Gathers for Author's Chair Sessions Don Graves and I discovered the importance of these sessions during our years as researchers with Ellen Blackburn Karelitz in her first-grade classroom. I wrote about them in the first edition of this book, and now I see Author's Chairs at all grade levels across this country. It's amazing.

Author's Chair sessions give students a chance to celebrate and/or request help. If the author shares a completed draft, the occasion bears similarity to a reading at the local bookstore when an author reads from her newly published book. After she reads to the assembled gathering, she calls on members of the audience to make comments and ask questions. I have learned a great deal from authors when readers have asked them about their books. I was amazed when I heard Sook Nyul Choi talk about *The Year of Impossible Goodbyes* (1991). In it she tells about her escape from North Korea under the barbed-wire fence. In real life, she tried twice unsuccessfully before finally succeeding, but in the book she wrote only about her final attempt. Authors always know much more than they put in their books.

Similarly, when children read from the Author's Chair, their classmates get the story behind and beyond the print. They ask questions, and the child who shares runs the show. The author fields the questions and comments about his work. This responsibility is part of what he expects to do when he volunteers to read. His teacher taught the authors what to do when they share and taught the members of the class what to do when they respond. The teacher shared from the Author's Chair many times and now her students know the procedure. They love to ask, "What is in your piece of writing that is different from what really happened?"

However, students share much more than their published works from the Author's Chair. They share the published work of professional authors, their classmates' writing, their teacher's writing, and their own drafts. These drafts may vary from portfolio reflections to writing tasks for science.

Teachers hold Author's Chair sessions every day, once a week, or at other intervals. When the group convenes, one person may share, three may share, or the clock may decide the length of the session. Both teacher and students conduct many mini-lessons in this setting.

Overall, the Author's Chair is a special chair. We all preserve that aspect of it.

Small Groups Meet to Confer About Their Work Whenever I ask my university classes for feedback on the workshops I create in my reading, writing, and evaluation courses, they say, "I learned so much when my small group met." Because I often have classes of only about fifteen people, and we frequently meet in a friendly circle, I used to undervalue small groups. It seemed to me that everyone participated in the class sessions and I thought they all learned a lot there.

However, for many people, a small group is the preferred setting in which to talk, and I now place increased value on small groups in my own teaching. The teachers count on them, and I schedule them regularly. In preparation for the class sessions during which their small groups will meet, the teachers think of questions to ask their groupmates or they choose something to share.

They bring their writing, reading, and/or portfolios. Each person takes a turn and shares whatever he wants response to at that time. Sometimes they are concerned about their teaching and sometimes about their work for our class. Hopefully these concerns and joys merge as they start to use, in their classrooms, ideas from our class. Often our course stimulates their own ideas and they go way beyond what I have envisioned.

Mark Milliken, an elementary teacher, created his own procedures. Over time, he began to place much more emphasis on small groups than he had early in his career. He used to worry about individual conferences. He couldn't get around to each student often enough to suit him, and he started to wonder if those conferences were appropriate. He heard himself do a lot of teaching in those settings and knew other students beyond the individual could benefit. Each conference could be a mini-lesson for students beyond the one he sat beside.

Over time, he abandoned individual conferences, and he now confers with individual students in group settings. Each student shares a draft and Mark and the others respond. The person who shares receives the benefit of diverse minds and the others learn more than his students did when they only met alone with Mark.

Regardless of how a teacher structures small groups, this venue can give students of all ages a chance to be heard with more assurance than in a large group.

Workers Celebrate Their Stretches in Mini-Lessons   When writers read, what do they do? This can be the topic of the mini-lessons for the year. The particulars of what the writers and readers in a classroom do when they read and write evolve from what they do when they gather 'round the Author's Chair, when they meet in small groups, when they work, and when they interact. One day in November 1999 as I interacted with first graders, I knelt beside David, whose paper looked like this:

Ittoafetre

I asked him to read it to me and he did: "I went to a fire truck." Of course! I could follow his words and print. We talked, and I learned that his father is a fireman. No wonder David was excited.

Then, because I knew that David needed to learn about spaces between words, but I didn't know if he were ready for that, I said, "I'll read you part of what I wrote today." I was carrying my writing with me as I circulated among the children, and I read, pointing to each word: "I walked into my new, empty, first-grade classroom and stood alone at Miss Rosedahl's desk."

Then I said, "Now you read yours to me again, and point to each word as you say it, like I did."

David did. I knew he understood the concept of a word, so I asked what he intended to write next.

"'And I went on it,'" he said.

As he started to write an *a* for *and*, I intervened. "Please put your finger after *truck* before you write the word *and*."

David did and soon started to write *I* without a space. Again, I reminded him of the space. As it turned out, I needed to remind him four times, and he spaced *it* by himself, a huge step for this young writer.

David's giant step forward was one possibility for a mini-lesson later that morning. Teachers often recognize students for their new accomplishments by using their work as the focus of a mini-lesson. As a teacher circulates during work time and listens during an Author's Chair session, she thinks about which child's stretch will make the most worthwhile lesson. She wants to teach something that (1) some of the children are ready to learn, (2) others need reinforced, and (3) has widespread application.

Mini-lessons typically arise from the students' work, rather than from textbooks or other commercial materials. We don't have to worry very much about students transferring a lesson to their own work when the new skills we share are already in their work. They can usually see the practicality of a skill, strategy, or process when someone in their midst has found it to be useful. In order to ensure the children's application of the mini-lessons to their work, some teachers extend them into the next day or even continue one for a week.

David's teacher could have done this. After the first day, when she and David showed his new accomplishment, he and his classmates could have brought children's literature in for the next day's mini-lesson. They could have counted the number of words in the first sentence of each book. In so doing, their awareness of the concept of a word would have increased. Next, in a lesson that may have spanned three days, the children could have each brought in two pieces of their own writing to show their growth. Some might have brought one in which they didn't use spaces and a more recent one in which they did. Others who always used spaces might have brought a piece of writing from the beginning of the school year and a more recent one to show something else they had learned.

This procedure fosters more mini-lessons. The children become detectives on the lookout for their stretches, for ideas for mini-lessons. These sessions help the students see themselves in forward motion and give them ideas of new skills to purposely try as writers.

At other times, the teacher uses her own writing to help students through a bottleneck. Tom Romano (2000) often uses his own writing and reading to help his students become aware of effective writing. I particularly like his section on dialogue (58–65) in which he gives two examples he has written to hilariously show effective talk. One addresses students' common desire to substitute synonyms for the word *said*, a situation I identified with immediately.

Romano also gives guidelines for dialogue, and he turns this mini-lesson designed for his students into one designed for adults, as well. Of the seven guidelines (Macauley & Lanning 1987), three are:

- It should sound spontaneous but avoid the repetitions of real talk.

- It should reveal something about the speakers' personalities.
- It should show relationships among people.

I think Romano's advice was particularly helpful to me at the moment I read it because only five minutes earlier I had been working on a draft about a visit with my grandma. It included much dialogue, and Romano's advice served me well, as I assumed it would. I know him and enjoy his writing. Students, too, regardless of age, appreciate lessons from their friends and know to whom to go when they need a refresher.

Hmmmm . . .

When Judy Fueyo, a friend of mine, was on sabbatical, she lived on Cape Cod, and took two art classes in Provincetown. Judy is a literacy professor, not a painter, but she decided to step into this new world during her leave so she could better understand its ties to writing. She sensed the importance of workshops to artists and wondered if participation in an artists workshop would give her insights into writing workshops for the K–12 teachers in the university classes she teaches.

Judy has become immensely excited about what she is learning. In both classes she participates in a weekly three-hour painting workshop. Her mode of expression in both is acrylics and this is the first time she has used them. As she had hoped, these workshops are joyful experiences that already mean much to her, both personally and professionally.

Personally, the immersion twice a week, and her work on other days in her newly created home workshop, have brought her to see her world in new ways. She sees shadows and light she had never noticed. Her study of professional painters and their works has helped her tremendously to see what she now appreciates in her friends' faces, her home, and the Cape. This will inform her writing, she trusts.

Professionally, Judy said, "One of the greatest fertilizers of work is talk and intermingling. It is so vital to have fellow artists to intensely talk about your ideas with." The artists workshops provide her with time to talk, move about, find momentum, and keep herself going.

Judy continued, "I can now work on a painting for more than an hour. When I started I was finished by the end of the first hour!"

"So, did you start another?" I asked.

"No! I walked around, just like a little kid in writers workshop. I looked at what everyone else was doing and I asked them questions. I learned, became excited, and got ideas. Now I can work for hours on one painting, but at first I had no idea what to do to continue to work on one."

All writing teachers have students who experience the dilemma Judy describes, but the availability of her diverse group working on their paintings helped Judy see possibilities in her own work. And the others became excited for her, the most in-experienced artist in the workshop. She started to create plans for herself.

"Jane, I finally have a plan!" she told me. "You know, for weeks I didn't have one. I had no idea what to plan, what could lie ahead, what I might do. Now I know enough about painting and about myself as a painter to create a plan. I'm on my way!"

It takes awhile for a writing workshop to work; it takes weeks for students of any age to know enough to create a plan that will move them forward. The workshop then serves a new function. Not only is it always the place in which writers and readers can find their stride, it becomes the space in which the enthusiasm of the others keeps each person going. Everyone is in this together.

Teachers' Roles

In the fall of 1999, two colleagues and I conducted a workshop on self-evaluation at the NCTE conference in Denver. We based it on one of the basic premises of writing workshops: they are public spaces in which writers work and learn from one another's work, as different from classrooms where students work alone in isolated desks in rows.

The three of us and the educators who attended the workshop devoted the day to discussions of who we are beyond our classrooms, who we are as teachers, and what our goals are. Our goals were public; we discussed them and what we intended to do to accomplish them.

To illustrate the public nature of goals, I shared my teaching goal for the graduate class on reading I had taught the previous spring:

> To receive a perfect score from this class on item 6 on the university's evaluation form. The last time I taught this class, my students ranked me lower on this item than on any other. It reads "Objectives for course were clearly presented."

Everyone in that reading class knew of my goal, and I kept asking them how I was doing.

The workshop participants laughed as they pictured the teachers in my class helping me teach them well.

I explained, "Everyone in the class knew everyone's goals—what we each wanted to learn about the teaching of reading—and we devoted our workshop time each week to serving as resources to each other. I, for example, kept asking, 'What are the objectives for this course?' If someone didn't know, I'd present them again in written, demonstration, visual, or oral form."

Setting goals is automatic for professional educators. Making them public, seeking help, and helping others can each be a challenge. Documenting and sharing the artifacts that show our growth and telling the accompanying stories are vital to the livelihood of our profession. The public must know that we are continuously and purposefully becoming more adept at our responsibilities.

In these times, unfortunately, some persons outside of education don't believe that we educators consciously grow; they see it as their responsibility to make decisions about what should be done to improve our work. Agencies and individuals at the federal, state, and local levels try to tell teacher educators and secondary and elementary teachers what and how to teach. We are enmeshed in a hierarchical system, with the locus of authority in Washington, D.C. That's where the money is. In order to secure funds, the U.S. Department of Education needs to speak in a strong voice when it asks for its rightful portion of the national budget. It asks for funds to support the teaching procedures the legislators understand.

If we want the teaching processes we favor to receive recognition, we must be sure our legislators believe in what we do. One of our roles is to create a public personae of ourselves as professionals who are articulate about what we do well and who have specific plans for our continuous growth.

We Strive to Become Better Teachers

The interns I supervise pursue teacher research within their internships. This helps them see, from day one, the central importance of their own professional development to their lives as teachers. Trisha Sutphen, who interned in a second grade, knows she still has a long way to go and that she will never perfect this art, but she does intend to devote her career to revising and polishing her teaching skills. She reflects on her teaching, celebrates when her days go well, and generates options for new beginnings when lessons flounder. Trish struggles and flourishes amidst the support of her colleagues.

When Trish began her yearlong, full-time internship she found it difficult to set a goal to purposely guide her growth. She was overwhelmed! In order to find a focus in the midst of turmoil, Trish studied two children as writers. Throughout the fall she conferred with each of them each week, taped the conferences, transcribed them, and wrote a weekly reflection about each one. Through these reflections, the meaning of teaching began to reveal itself to Trish.

She wrote about Mark in the following way:

> Well, from looking at Mark's writing now, compared to what it was at our last conference, it is plain to see that he has lost interest in his Cub Scouts draft. Besides the fact that he has written only two lines, he has planted a big THE END at the end of his short piece of writing. . . . I am disappointed that my last conference did not have much effect and concerned that Mark is, once again, abandoning a topic. . . .

Trish evaluated her efforts with Mark, brought her confessions to the seminar I held with the interns each week, and our group supported her efforts. Trish continued on her relentless search and re-search for ways to find out what Mark needed. She had taken her first steps on a long trek toward understanding that it can be hard for writers to be able to recognize events and issues in their lives about which they feel strongly enough to write with energy. Trish was learning that no formula existed for her to follow; while some of her students wrote volumes, Mark wrote two lines.

For each of our weekly seminar sessions, Trish created a two-part portfolio entry about one of her two case study children. Her artifact was usually a draft written by one of the students or a portion of a transcript of a conference she had held, and in her reflection she repeatedly addressed her goal, or research question: "What do I say in a conference to be as helpful as possible to the writer?"

Although the interns and I all conducted different kinds of research, each of us prepared for our seminars by setting aside time to stop and evaluate what we were learning. Trish constantly critiqued herself, her students, and her profession. She was not searching for the *right* way to teach, nor for a foolproof way. The interns' goals gave them a place to center their ultrabusy lives and document an accomplishment on the road of ever-better teaching.

During their second semester, most of the interns set a new goal for themselves. Whereas their emphases varied, the main focus was on the two-week unit each of them was required to create and conduct. Trish had decided in the fall that her unit would be on poetry, and she had read Georgia Heard's (1989) *For the Good of the Earth and the Sun* and Don Graves' (1994) *A Fresh Look at Writing*. She had learned that it is wise to marinate children in poetry, so, during the fall, she had frequently read poetry to the students for their enjoyment and placed several poetry books in their classroom library. Some children had chosen to read them during reading workshop.

As the time for her unit approached, Trish set an overall goal for it, "What encourages, supports, and enriches children's love for poetry?" She arrived at this question after much deliberation (Hubbard & Power 1999) and officially began her unit—which she designed as a seven-week unit—during a week in February.

During those five days, Trish focused each day on one way to sweep children into poetry, such as by moving their bodies to the beat of poems or by choral reading. These sessions opened reading workshop each day that week.

Trish taped all of these class sessions, transcribed them, and wrote a reflection about each. All went well, and none were perfect; she planned to revise all of them the next time she taught poetry. Here, for example, is part of her analysis of the day of the choral readings:

> When I told the class that we were going to read some poems out loud there was cheering and "Yesss!!"-ing from the kids. I was very happy that they were so excited. . . . Then I invited them to read "Potato Chips" by M. C. Livingston with me. . . . Sarah noticed the words *munching*, *lunching*, and *crunching*. . . .
>
> Next, I began explaining that we were going to read the poem using two voices . . . a third section crunched as loudly as possible on a handful of potato chips. . . . Unfortunately, it was getting incredibly late and we had to move on to something else before everyone had a chance to be in the chip-cruncher group. *That* was when the true disappointment set in. I should have planned my time much more carefully. One of our students is a boy with autism and he was totally unable to handle the disappointment. . . .

Again, as in the fall when she had reflected on her writing conferences, Trish analyzed what went well and what could have been better. Her daily reflections and her weekly written reflections for our seminar helped ensure an awareness of the importance of both reflection and support in order for her career to thrive. At the end of her unit, Trish felt satisfied, overall, about her children's love of poetry, but her questions about the child with autism lingered, and that's fine. All professionals find themselves driven by more questions.

At the end of our year, the interns created portfolios to take with them when they went out for job interviews. Each organized this document differently, and Trish decided to use her philosophical statement as her guiding principle. Each section in it became a section in her portfolio, including Writing Workshop, Assessment, and Meeting the Needs of Teachers.

Trish interviewed for a position as a third-grade teacher, and the element of her portfolio that most impressed the principal and teachers who interviewed her was her series of reflections. She had included detailed, pagelong reflections to accompany every item in her portfolio, and the principal took Trish's portfolio home for a weekend to read it carefully. This principal wanted to promote purposeful, deliberate growth on the part of her faculty and saw Trish as a person who did this. Trish had gained a relatively clear image of herself as a professional. The principal offered Trish the position and she accepted.

Trish initially learned about reflection when she studied writing instruction. She thought about what worked and what didn't. She didn't mechanically teach one lesson after another. Trish could tell us what she was learning to do as a teacher and what she was working on to become better. To look at herself with appreciation and scrutiny is her goal for her professional life.

We Find Out Who Our Students Are

The more we know about the overall lives of our students, the more likely we are to be able to help them with their schoolwork. There may be lots of aspects of our students we could learn about, but I will write about two: who they are in school and who they are beyond school.

Who Our Students Are In School   We purposefully create the culture of a school. Ideally, it is one in which our students benefit from their entire day.

When I taught at Hanahauoli, a private day school in Honolulu, I experienced a well-crafted milieu. The parents, teachers, and children had created a Deweyian culture years before my tenure there, during the heyday of John Dewey in the 1920s. A group of parents designed this school where the children continue to participate in many projects. In order to do so, they use the resources of a music teacher, a rhythm teacher, and a shop teacher. A separate building houses a shop in which the students construct the mosaic school sign and create the stepping stones that crisscross campus.

My first-grade classroom included an annex equipped with an enormous supply of blocks and a puppet stage. We had our own sandbox. I found out who my students were within a multitude of locations and experiences. When I saw Peter create phenomenal block structures in the annex, intricate roadways in the sandbox, and detailed cars in shop, I could eventually find reading and writing tasks that fueled his passions. The more I knew, the greater the likelihood I could get my students started on the right foot.

I also taught second grade at Hanahauoli and tailored math assignments to my various students. In handwriting, I helped each child with the letter(s) he needed to work on. My children didn't have assigned seats; they sat at whichever cluster of desks felt right at that moment. All of this was new to me. In my previous teaching positions, I had taught group lessons, and my students had sat in assigned seats, but at Hanahauoli I learned to more carefully honor my students as individuals with varying needs (Tanner 1997).

At the same time, they knew one another well; my students had been together since prekindergarten and would remain together through sixth grade in this little school with only one section of each grade level. The individualized nature of instruction did not keep them apart. They cared about one another and helped one another a great deal with their work. In addition, because I knew what each needed and could do, I knew who to send to the courtyard when fidgety Tommy needed a reading partner. The school was a community of children and adults who were committed to the well-being of this place.

Unfortunately, schools exist in which the culture turns children's dreams into nightmares. Denny Taylor, Debbie Coughlin, and Joanna Marasco (1997) edited a book in which they show the shattered dreams of students who found themselves in the wrong school at the wrong time. One of those students, Mark, written about by LaFon Phillips (46–68), did not pass sixth grade because his work habits were poor. He had test scores above the grade 6 level, but his teacher awarded him failing grades on his report card because of poor effort. His mother, the author and a teacher herself, and father, a professor, unsuccessfully fought the system. The culture of a school wields power and it is our responsibility to exert the power in support of the children. When we know them, we must use our overall knowledge to serve them well.

Who Our Students Are Beyond School On Bromley Mission in Liberia, as a Peace Corps volunteer, I was different from all of my students, and I learned the value of us learning as much as possible about each other's total lives. My first and second graders spent at least an hour at my house every afternoon. I learned to sort out the difference between a play ma, a real ma, and a born ma. They learned that it was impossible to plait my hair. The Bromley community was close; we all—teachers and students—lived on campus. Everyone knew one another's family stories. Each person counted; no one got lost in the shuffle of schoolwork or life. Everyone helped everyone, and a few of us still do, decades later.

However, it took me years to realize that it isn't only in Africa that it behooves me to understand the influence of students' lives on my work as their teacher. In 1990 some of us UNH researchers trekked down Route 101 to Manchester at the request of Jane Kearns, the director of writing for the city. We didn't focus on one school; we studied with a few teachers who taught at various elementary and secondary schools all located near the center of the city, where the statistics showed the highest free lunch count, etc. The teachers jumped in with both feet; excitement reigned. We were about to learn about *students as evaluators of themselves as readers and writers* in a culture quite different from that of the schools near UNH.

At the beginning, we didn't realize the importance of the students' lives beyond school. We focused on school. We asked the students to create portfolios to show themselves as readers and writers. Many of them did, but some didn't. From those who claimed to not be readers and writers I learned the most (Hansen 1996b). When a student does not see herself as a writer, it is impossible for her to become a better writer. The same goes for reading. These students needed to see themselves as readers and writers before they could go further.

It took us months to realize that it was the students' lives beyond school that would permit them and us to see them as readers and writers. One student who didn't see himself as a reader in school brought the floor plan of the Boys Club he went to after school every day. He could read it! Gradually, as word spread, students found evidence of themselves as readers and writers outside of school and brought the artifacts inside. They could read old license plates and could teach others. Gradually, as they shared and gained confidence, they took the reading and writing of additional classmates seriously and accepted invitations to try additional forms of literacy. They were reading and writing in school. Eventually, with the support of their classmates and teachers, they purposefully became better readers and writers.

Similar evolutions occur in other schools. Maureen Barbieri (1995) wrote about an entire year she devoted to helping her grade 6 girls see themselves as competent young women whose thoughts deserved recognition. While they were on the track toward becoming unassertive young women only seeking to please others, she helped them find situations in which their voices carried influence. Maureen taught them to critique their white, middle-class culture and find ways to step out of it.

Students' lives outside of school provide them with a springboard into reading and writing in ways we don't understand but strive to learn (Ladson-Billings 1994). When their cultures become classroom currency, they can critique, question, and consciously seek value in who they are. And, knowledge of who they are helps us find ways to get them started as writers and readers.

We Find Out What Our Students Know

The process of finding out what our students know in order to know what to teach them next is a hallmark of what we do as reading and writing teachers (Daniel 1996). This distinguishes us from teachers of the past who picked up their red pens to search for what their students did not know and taught the next lesson in the textbook regardless. The same goes for reading teachers. We have stopped highlighting mistakes on children's work and then assigning them the next page in the workbook just because it's there. Instead, we listen to them read and talk. While they are in the process of reading and talking, we listen for what they know, in order to know what they are on the verge of knowing, in order to teach the very process or skill they are ready to learn.

Recently I listened to three very different children in one grade 1 classroom in Nassau, Bahamas. Richanda read from a little book: "The Dog. The dog has red ears. The dog has red paws." She read fluently and could also read the words in isolation, in random order. I needed to listen to her more so I could discover her growing edge. Then I'd know what to do to help her become a better reader. Maybe she needed to read from a more difficult text in order to grow.

Next I sat beside Tishea, who read the same lines about the dog. She also read fluently, but when I asked her to point to certain words, she couldn't. I asked her to read her name, Tishea Brown, and she did. I asked her to point to *Brown*, and she could. She could also point to *Tishea*. She sat on the verge of knowing the concept of a word, so I decided to try to teach her this skill. With minimal help she learned to point to various words in the two sentences she could read. As Tishea continues to learn to see individual words she will not need to memorize and can read longer text. By sitting beside her while she read, I learned what she knew.

Finally I moved to Trevornicka, and she read the first of the two sentences about the dog. *Has* was difficult for Trevornicka, who preferred to say *have*. We read it together a few times with minimal success and Trevornicka diverted herself from this hard work by touching my hair and saying to her classmates at large, "I never see a woman with soft hair like that before. Come, feel her hair." Several of the little Bahamian children instantly encircled me, feeling my hair. One said, "I don't cry when my hair get plait." Another said, "Her hair soft, soft." When the children dispersed, Trevornicka returned to her little book, I taught her to read the first sentence fluently, and she went right on to read the second sentence correctly on her own on her first try.

I found out how difficult this language pattern was for her, and wondered if I had done the right thing when I insisted that she read it the printed way. Later, when I talked with several Bahamian teachers, I asked if they would have focused on this language difficulty and they said yes. Children learn to talk and read at the same time. Other children struggled with *has* and practiced with Trevornicka, who needed to practice this new speech pattern.

I learned to closely study students when they read after I learned to carefully watch and listen to them when they write. Not only did I notice how carefully young writers focus on meaning, I noticed this similar behavior when these young writers read the print others created. In order to ensure carryover from writing to reading, teachers use similar teaching processes in both writing and reading. Thus, when Trevornicka writes, if she confuses *has/have*, her teacher will refer her to the story about the red dog. Students' reading and writing can inform each other when we know the details of what they can do in each.

Hmmmm . . .

Christine Duthie (1996) wrote about the autobiography unit she conducted with her first-grade children. When they talked about the books she read to them, they thought about their past and future experiences. On the last day of school, as they talked about their next school year, one child said, "Next year I'm gonna be a friend to someone who looks scared on the first day of school . . . like, remember the boy who was blind in that book?" This young child saw herself as part of a larger culture that isn't always kind, but could be. Christine had purposefully taught her young students to see themselves as persons who care throughout their school day.

The processes of evaluation, writing, reading, and talk can help students create supportive cultures, and they need many opportunities to do so. Euro-American students and teachers, whose culture has dominated our country and educational system for centuries, especially need to take a close look at the gatekeeper role we play so well. We need to seriously consider whom we welcome in and whom we don't. Finding out as much as we can about the culture of the outsiders will help us know the terrain in which these students negotiate their lives.

Many Euro-American students in classes with students from other countries think, "I don't have a culture," which may show their unawareness of their prejudices and viewpoints. Self-study is especially important for the gatekeepers of a culture (Florio-Ruane 1994). Boys can critique the wide freeway their male culture oftentimes affords them, gifted students can critique their privileges, and children who don't ordinarily approach new students can purposefully do so.

As teachers, we constantly critique our classrooms, our schools, and our selves in our effort to move forward. Our involvement in writing has helped us realize the importance of strong voices in our efforts. We challenge ourselves to strengthen our own voices as we fulfill one of our primary roles—to cocreate with our students school cultures in which everyone supports learners.

Students' Roles |

Twelve

Many students' roles in school are complicated by life. Christina, in grade 5, commented on her own worries, "Violence is not in my family. It's just outside wherever we live." She thought about this violence, and her worries affected her schoolwork.

When school started, Christina's teacher, Jim Pottle, shared artifacts and written reflections about his out-of-school life as his way to introduce himself. He invited the students to do likewise, and Christina brought in many artifacts to show her family life, especially pictures of her father, who had died. She stood before the class and shared all of them but hadn't written about them.

One day Pat Aichele, the researcher in her room, joined a portfolio-sharing group that included Christina. Each person in the group shared a story, as it turned out, of a death in his or her family. One student had written a three-paragraph expression of love about her grandfather who died that past summer. Christina still hadn't written, but she talked about her father, showed his picture, and said how much she missed him. "This was a very emotional group share for all of us," Pat said. "We've all been close since then."

After that group session, Christina began to write several memoirs about her father and her family. When she shared one of them she said, "In my other school I didn't have any friends. I'm Puerto Rican and I'm too fat, so kids made fun of me. Here, in this school, I have friends and I like coming to school." One of the things Pat Aichele did to validate Christina was try to speak Spanish with her, as did others, which Christina appreciated.

Below I relate parts of a note Christina wrote to Pat:

Dear Mrs. A,

> I like it when you take me to share my portfolio because you understand me and you really like to hear my stories and you like to see what I put in my portfolio and thank you. . . . I love you a lot because you and Mr. Pottle are very good to me but I know I did some things wrong. I admit. But, what I saw when I was small where I lived was a lot of violence, but that's the way I learned how to grow up.

Christina tried to sort out many roles. She wondered what to do when violence occurred and what this meant she was to do as she grew up. Initially, Christina wondered about her place in this new class but eventually shared information about her family with her classmates. Eventually, she created a separate portfolio, titled ¡La Familia Siempre¡ *(The Family Always),* just for artifacts about her family, and two other portfolios—one for artifacts from classmates and one for her schoolwork. Through her reflections about math, her teacher learned that Christina did not feel challenged. She was bored with the pace. He wrote, "This is a valid need. I will consider more appropriate problems for you."

The adults in this room expected Christina and her classmates to play roles new to Christina. She was not used to writing about her work and having her teacher respond. It was new for her to listen to her classmates and teachers explore the meanings of their lives and to support their emotional needs. In this new role as listener, Christina learned to seek information from others, as they solicited information from her.

She was not used to telling her stories, much less writing them. But Christina took on the role of writer when her fears about the wrongs she had committed were overshadowed by her belief that her new classmates and teachers understood her. The roles her teacher expected her to play enabled Christina to create a space for herself amidst her new classmates.

In other classrooms (Schwartz 2000) students actually include their family members when they write, which helps some of them write and tell their stories in great detail. From these experiences, they can start their treks as learners.

Students Find Something to Learn

In Karen Boettcher's sixth-grade, Armen initially did not attract our attention. When the boys brought in artifacts in answer to the question "Who am I?," he brought comics, and others brought Lego directions, drawings of knife collections, and sports articles.

Girls brought karate photos, gifts from relatives, and notes from friends. Girls showed themselves as learners by comparing pieces of writing they had saved from earlier years with current writing, by listing titles of progressively harder books, and with book order blanks—one girl now ordered more books than she had in previous years, for example.

Boys hadn't saved as much work from previous years but did place long pieces of writing in their portfolios (longer than anything they had previously written), copies of book jackets ("This is the first entire book I've read"), and, again, Lego directions ("I read every word").

During the fall semester, Armen portrayed himself as an athlete and outgoing leader. All of his classmates liked him. He produced nothing, however, to show any particular academic potential he saw in himself.

By contrast, most of the students' evaluations led them to the point where they challenged themselves as readers and writers. They loved their new reading program in which they learned, for the first time in their careers, how to choose what they read. They also enjoyed various aspects of choice within writing and collected evidence of their growth for their portfolio entries, purposely trying new things so they could show evidence of their growth, set goals, and create plans.

Armen didn't outwardly oppose the system, but he didn't take off. He became frustrated. He knew he was supposed to find something to write about that he loved, but what? His teacher wanted to catch this young man before something else did. As it turned out, the ongoing policy of bringing in significant artifacts turned the tide.

For Christmas Armen received a book of poetry by Edgar Allan Poe from his dad. He brought it to class, shared one poem as a dramatic reading, put it in his portfolio for easy access, and wrote about its importance to him. He then started to write his own poetry and shared it over the next several days on various occasions with the class and informally with his friends. Then, one by one, various boys in the class started to venture into poetry. Armen gladly lent them his Poe book, and they read others from the classroom and school library. As they composed, they started to share line by line as they wrote: "Hey, listen to this."

Many poets were born, and Armen saw himself as a writer with potential—and as a reader. Three conditions allowed this to happen: (1) The students chose the forms they wanted to pursue during reading and writing. (2) Each student purposely tried to place himself in the position of a learner. (3) The atmosphere invited them to closely link themselves in a public way to their work. I will briefly address each of these points.

First, the students pursued, during reading and writing, the forms they chose. This is not to say that Karen never gave specific assignments, but as part of her writing-reading curriculum, the students kept books of their choice and writing of their choice ongoing. Reading and writing, for these students, often influenced each other, as Armen's excitement about poetry did. He both read and wrote it. Their evaluations of themselves as readers and writers often dovetailed, as did their goals, plans, and portfolio documentations.

In order to keep this complexity alive, Karen set aside long blocks of time for her students to work on their goals. In so doing, she showed the students that she honored what they valued. They had time to become engrossed in their books and in their writing. This commitment of time underscores the notion of *students as evaluators*. These students knew that their teacher placed significance on what they valued.

Second, each student tried to place himself in the position of a learner. They tried to find something they felt excited about to work on during writing and reading. That was their responsibility. The task was more than simply "I have to choose a book to read and a topic to write about." The task was "I want to find something new to try as a reader and as a writer—something that is interesting to me." Karen helped in any way she could. In Armen's case, she urged him to read a poem to the class and then casually—and very purposefully—wondered aloud, "Have you ever considered writing poetry, Armen?"

He took off, and his friends followed. Karen's role became that of the questioner who kept the boys active as evaluators. She repeatedly, whenever appropriate during a class discussion, during group time, or in a conference, asked questions such as these:

> What is good about this poem?
> What did you try that was new for you?
> What are you putting in your portfolio as evidence of your growth?
> What will you try next?

Finally, the atmosphere invited them to closely link themselves, in a public way, to their work. Whereas students in any classroom may bring Christmas gifts to school after the holidays, the ever-present portfolios in this classroom made it more likely that connections between those gifts and schoolwork could be drawn. These students had shared a wide array of items and Armen's book of poetry from his dad was very apropos. The dramatic reading was not an extraordinary mode of presentation in this particular classroom. Karen regularly expressed herself with gesture and a stage voice. Keeping various possibilities open helped the students find a comfortable way to become engaged and engage others.

The students regularly saw their own potential in the work of their friends and pushed themselves forward. Whereas they did talk about what they had done, it was their plans that excited them. The answers to the questions "What are you going to do next?" or "What should I do next?" or, to one's self, "I wonder what to try next?" revealed the overzealous excitement of some, the realistic plans of many, and the hesitant forward steps of others.

People learn best when their work comes from within, when they are committed. We may train students, condition them, even coerce them, but without commitment, they learn to a lesser degree. We help students act with conviction by freeing them to be who they are; we want Christina to feel comfortable with her exploration of violence and Armen to feel comfortable with his poetry. Deliberately reflecting on who they are, they can work intentionally to become the selves they envision.

This is a difficult task. Many students begin new school years with low expectations for themselves, and their teachers must perform herculean tasks to create classrooms in which the many voices become interested listeners who are curious about others and look at themselves in wonderment. Eventually, sometimes after several months, they find something they want to learn.

Students Learn New Information

For students to *find something to learn* is an extension of *choose your own book* in reading and *choose your own topic* in writing. In a writing workshop students use writing, reading, and sharing to learn about something of interest to them, whether it be Edgar Alan Poe, a Puerto Rican grandfather, or what *the state of New Hampshire is doing to preserve the Old Man in the Mountain* (the state symbol). Choosing your own topic is more complicated than we used to think.

Saying "find something to learn" sounds new because, in part, we often viewed writing workshops through narrow lenses when we originally created them. We often saw them as places in which students wrote personal narratives about their own experiences. Whereas this writing is significant and is the kind of writing that brought Christina into the world of writing, we now know that it's important to include many kinds of writing and reading in a workshop. Writers who have been affected by death may do research about J. C. Penney's, the company Grandfather worked for throughout his life, or they may read about other young people who have lost treasured family members and write poetry.

Some students learn about their topics by conducting interviews in the Puerto Rican neighborhood, writing travel articles for the local newspaper, and writing travel brochures about Puerto Rico. In order to do so, they study and must learn a great deal. Often, writing topics are interests about which to read and learn in as many ways as possible. The students pursue their passions, write, and ask questions.

The fifth-grade students in Laurie Swistak's classroom in Newport, Rhode Island (Allen 2001), travel a complicated, rewarding journey as they learn about topics they have chosen within a *multigenre unit* Laurie creates. Her students write, talk, research, create art, and read about a person or historical event of their choice. Whereas there are many processes students may use to learn about the topics to which they are committed, the multigenre projects these students pursue (Romano 1995) provide many opportunities by which they can learn. And, the students become so excited!

These projects are collages of writing and artistic expression with an overarching theme that consumes the creators and readers. Laurie devotes three months of language arts instruction from late January through April to these particular projects, and even though children often want to study animals, she has found in the three years during which her students have created multigenre projects that animals don't provide as many possibilities for exploration as people (Graves 1999) and historical events. So, she asks each student to choose an event or a person to learn about.

Whereas their active study takes place from January to April, Laurie devotes the entire fall to preparation for this extensive unit. The students have heard about these projects from their friends, and she brainstorms possible topics with them, stressing that they eventually will each select a topic in which they are intensely interested. They also engage in a poetry unit and a newspaper unit, two genres they may incorporate into their multigenre projects. In addition they analyze fiction, another genre they may find helpful.

During the twelve weeks of the project, the class meets for language arts every day. On Wednesdays Laurie sets aside about twenty minutes to clarify any concerns they have, a valuable time to preserve. The following schedule is the current one they use for the overall unit:

Week

One   Poetry and song: ten-minute writes.

Two   Fiction and character studies.

Three Nonfiction and goals: What question(s) do you want to answer about your person or event?

Four   Research visit to a nearby university. Multimedia opportunities.

Five   Class creates evaluation criteria. Weekly assignment sheets. Study of past multigenre papers.

Six   References. Workshop.

Week

Seven   Workshop.

Eight   Workshop. Editing. Creative arts.

Nine   Workshop. Editing.

Ten   Oral presentation skills.

Eleven   Practice presentations.

Twelve   Presentations.

Their weekly assignment sheets help keep them on track, as they each decide what they plan to accomplish that week, in relation to their own goals and the overall schedule. These sheets require each student to write out specific plans.

Laurie is considering having the students keep process journals in which they would record the process they undergo while they are learning about their topics. Her mentor, Camille Allen, a professor at Salve Regina University, has her college students keep process journals during the creation of their multigenre projects and finds them invaluable. At the end, each student has not only a finished product but also a record of what he did along the way, such as how he analyzed his notes, generated his genres, contemplated ways to incorporate the arts, and involved friends.

Each fifth grader does keep a resource notebook with three sections. The first contains examples of many types of genres such as advice columns, front page headlines, crossword puzzles, ballads, limericks, metaphors, and narratives. These many models of writing serve as a quick reference for them when they are creating their various genres, all of which shed light and show perspectives on their people or events. The second section is for their drafts, and the third is a folder with pockets where they keep their notes, printouts, data from interviews (Rogovin 1998), and other information they collect.

During the three years she has conducted these projects with her classes, Laurie has learned to designate a place in the room where the students may store all resource materials. This helps the learners who easily misplace materials.

At all times throughout the fall and during the twelve weeks of immersion in January through April, the students evaluate their progress; they talk about what they want to learn, how they might go about it, when they goofed, and when they succeeded. These continual conversations are similar to those that occur across the day in many classrooms when students are learning to read books in first grade and write narratives about their families in any grade. Knowing how to go about learning something is the hallmark of a learner, as it is the lifesaver of a writer. In many studies of writing over the last few decades we have learned to teach writers as much as possible about writing, so they know which writing processes are available to them. Then they can choose effective strategies in order to use writing to learn about something they want to understand.

Students Document What They Learn

Viewing documentation as a responsibility of students is new for many of us. Students can create and maintain the records of their growth. Moving at least some of that task to the students helps them scrutinize more carefully what they have learned, are doing, and are learning.

Students can keep lists of their reading-writing proficiencies, reading-writing connections they have found, books they've read and writing they've composed, and genres of reading and writing they have read and written (Hansen 1997; see Figures 12-1 through 12-4).

Oftentimes, the most important documentation is the examples of work the children collect. When first grader Stephanie decides to put a paper about eggs in her portfolio because it shows her best handwriting, she circles the words she thinks show her best printing. Then she writes her reflection: "These are my best letters m p t c." Stephanie's self-evaluation is very different from a contrasting act in which her teacher might have circled the best examples and written a note to Stephanie. For Stephanie to circle her own exemplary letters and write her own reflection gives her much practice at critical thinking and evaluation.

Diane Conway's children take home their accumulated documentation at designated times throughout the year, and she expects them each to arrange a time to sit beside an adult and carefully share their collections. They practice this in school. Then, the adult writes a note to the child in which he tells the child what he appreciates in the child's depiction of herself as a learner. When Diane's children carried their portfolios home for the first time, she labored over the cover letter in which she invited the children's caregivers to write these notes. It was extremely important for them to respond positively to the children's collections. Also, she wanted to make sure the family knew how precious the portfolios were, so they would help the children remember to return them. She wrote:

November 14

Dear Parents,

Today the children are bringing home their portfolios. These portfolios are the places for each of them to show who they are as a person and a learner. The children have worked hard at collecting artifacts that show who they are, what kinds of things they like, and

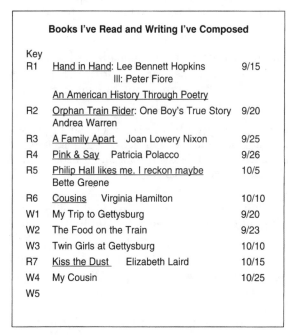

List of Reading-Writing Proficiencies
My dates and book/writing

1.	Paragraphs for new speakers	W3	10/10
2.	Commas in a series	W2	9/23
3.	Connections between books	R2	9/25
		R3	
4.	Use graphic feature to locate information	W1	9/20
5.	Understand that one book may elicit a variety of responses	R3	9/25
6.	Listen and respond thoughtfully to others	9/14 Class Share. Doug's writing. (see journal)	
7.	Choose a form appropriate to the purpose for writing		
8.			

Figure 12-1. A list of reading-writing proficiencies.

Reading/Writing Connections

9/20	I used four lines from "The Gettysburg Address" (p. 63, Hopkins) in my poem (W1)
9/25	Books 2 & 3 are on the same topic. I never heard of Orphan Trains before!
10/10	I used ideas/ways to write from Greene and Nixon in W3. I used questions to end chapters like Nixon sometimes did. I used months for chapters like Greene did.
10/27	

Figure 12-2. A record of reading-writing connections.

Books I've Read and Writing I've Composed

Key		
R1	Hand in Hand: Lee Bennett Hopkins Ill: Peter Fiore	9/15
	An American History Through Poetry	
R2	Orphan Train Rider: One Boy's True Story Andrea Warren	9/20
R3	A Family Apart Joan Lowery Nixon	9/25
R4	Pink & Say Patricia Polacco	9/26
R5	Philip Hall likes me. I reckon maybe Bette Greene	10/5
R6	Cousins Virginia Hamilton	10/10
W1	My Trip to Gettysburg	9/20
W2	The Food on the Train	9/23
W3	Twin Girls at Gettysburg	10/10
R7	Kiss the Dust Elizabeth Laird	10/15
W4	My Cousin	10/25
W5		

Figure 12-3. A record of reading and writing.

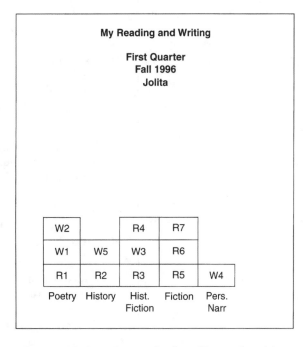

My Reading and Writing

First Quarter
Fall 1996
Jolita

Poetry	History	Hist. Fiction	Fiction	Pers. Narr
W2		R4	R7	
W1	W5	W3	R6	
R1	R2	R3	R5	W4

Figure 12-4. A record of reading and writing genres.

what they are learning. They are proud of their portfolios and can't wait to share them with you.

Please try to set aside 20–30 minutes to go through the portfolio with your child. After your child shares this portfolio, I'd appreciate it if you could take the time to write a short note or comment for your child to keep in the portfolio. In the note, you might want to tell your son or daughter what you liked or what you learned from seeing the portfolio.

Because we use the portfolios every day, it's important that they come back to school on Wednesday. Please help your child to remember this portfolio Wednesday morning.

Thank you for your help.

Sincerely,
Ms. Conway

The parents' response was "phenomenal," wrote Carol Wilcox (the researcher in Diane's class) for one of our meetings. Seventeen out of eighteen students returned the portfolios the next morning, and each child had shared with a mom, a dad, an aunt, or a grandparent. About half the adults wrote notes, and those responses were overwhelmingly positive and encouraging. Gerry's mom wrote:

> I really enjoyed looking at your portfolio with you. It's nice to know who your best friend is. I already knew you wanted to be a fireman, and as always, it makes me proud. I loved your drawings and am always very, very proud of how smart you are. I'm proud to have you as my son.

Tyler's mother didn't write a note to him. Instead, he became so excited while the two of them looked at his portfolio that he wanted to dictate additional information about himself for her to write, and she decided to let Tyler's words serve as her response:

> I like it when me and mommy go to the Dairy Queen to get ice cream. I like it when me and Mommy read books together. I like it when Kyle, Mommy, Denny and I read prayers before bed. When I grow up I would like to be a Power Ranger.

Many of the family members wrote notes that included both Diane and the child. Shannon's aunt wrote this comment for her portfolio:

> I like the parts when she wrote on her own. It shows she really wants to learn how to read and write. Keep up the good work, Shannon. You're learning fast.

The collections provided a forum around which the families could have positive conversations about their children's schoolwork and the portfolios provided a place for parents to teach Diane about their children:

I thought Daniel's portfolio was really neat. He did a good job and he's starting to read really well. Daniel will be going for his orange belt in karate next Saturday. He's doing really well in karate.

The two of them added a couple of new artifacts—photos of Daniel playing baseball and doing karate.

When Karen Boettcher's sixth graders brought their portfolios home, they wrote the letters to their parents and each created a final page for their portfolios labeled "What do you think of my portfolio?" with three columns: date, name, and comments. Most of the parents wrote specific, personal comments, such as:

- You have quite an imagination. I like the way you describe the class's reaction on going on the field trip.
- My favorite thing in the portfolio was the story "Ghost." It really made me laugh. My surprise was to find out that I was admired by you. It made me feel ten feet tall!
- I liked his portfolio because it constantly shows growth and a bright future.

The portfolios started an ongoing cycle in which the students and their parents continually asked the questions "Who am I? Who is my child? What shows who my child is?"

In January, before Ms. Conway's first graders took home their portfolios, she asked each child to show and tell how she or he had changed as a writer. Most children found more than one piece of writing and used them to show their growth, but Jake created three for a new entry (see Figure 12-5). Note the placement of the numbers 1, 2, and 3.

Jake wrote the following as his reflection, or self-evaluation:

1. Ths is the way I usee To Draw Ninja.
2. Ths is how I Drew ThM Nexs.
3. This is the way Draw Now.

Diane was impressed by Jake's ability to draw figures that matched his development and to articulate his growth. The daily conversations in her classroom help the children see themselves as learners with a future, as shown by their responses on this form, which they fill out about once a month. In February, many children named writing or reading as what they were proud of and the other—writing or reading—as what they still wanted to learn. Jake, however, wrote the following:

I'm good at <u>drawing</u>.
I want to get better at <u>writing karate people</u>.

Jake wrote with both words and pictures but preferred pictures. He wanted to get even better at drawing, his passion. It was in his drawings that he measured his growth.

1. Ths is the way I use To Draw Ninja.

2. Ths is how I Drew ThM Nexs.

3. This is the way Draw Now.

Figure 12-5. Jake's self-evaluation.

Later in February, when Diane asked the children to prepare their portfolios for another home showing, she again told them to compare old writing from the beginning of the year with current writing and to write a reflection. Jake now evaluated himself in terms of his written words: "I used to write short now I write longer."

For the child, parents, and teacher to observe the means by which each child shows himself as a learner adds a great deal to what we know when we only use grades and/or show children through adult eyes (Jervis 1996). The children's voices count. For decades we have worked hard to create writing workshops in which writers write in distinctive voices, and now we know how much assurance these voices receive when their reading and evaluation programs also feature their own voices (Stires 2000).

Teachers elsewhere (Lenski, Riss, & Flickinger 1996) create student-led conferences in school. A teacher in one of my classes did this, and each child led his or her parents through his or her own portfolio. In this case, each portfolio contained seven sections: out-of-school, school beyond my classroom, my personality, math, language, social studies, and science. Some parents stayed for a long time, discovering for the first time the true nature of their children. One parent said, "I *never* imagined my son knew what he knows."

In our six years of research on students as evaluators in Manchester, we never received a parent complaint about the documentation their children created. Real work and their children's perceptions of themselves provided invaluable data to supplement report cards.

One third grader went so far as to wonder, "What are grades for, anyway?"

His friend answered, "They're like portfolios but they don't tell as much."

Hmmmm . . .

At the beginning of a year in Karen Boettcher's sixth grade I interviewed students to gain their perceptions of themselves as readers. I wanted to know what they would say when they evaluated themselves.

Karen distributed an interest survey that provided me with a starting point for my interviews. In answer to "something you are known for," Keisha wrote, "I'm a good student." I asked if she had always been a good student or had become one only recently. She replied, "Always. I got straight A's all the way through first, second, and third grades."

Sarah, whom I interviewed separately, had written the same response, so, similarly, I asked her about being a good student. She sat for a minute and then said, "It started in third grade when I got my first A."

The answers of these two girls reinforced for me the need for students to become self-evaluators. These good students placed their self-judgment on teachers' grades, not on their own knowledge of what they could do. For their portfolios, Keisha and Sarah began to write reflections about examples that documented what they were doing to challenge themselves. They learned to be specific about what it means to be good, and they learned to see themselves as learners. They found new territory to learn about, such as how to read and write plays, and they documented their new expertise.

When students know themselves as learners, they have become good students.

Skills Readers and Writers Use Thirteen

I limp along with a heavy shoulder bag, and my students fear what I will find inside. A drama starts to unfold. Many call it a tragedy, an American tragedy, I guess. This thought—"I have papers to correct"—has gotten our profession in serious trouble.

We may know why. *When writers read*, they study the craft of the writer; they look for what they can use. The teacher who writes does this. When she has a bunch of her students' papers in her bag, she says, "I have papers to read."

What a difference! This writer studies the craft of these many writers; she looks for what they can learn from one another when they share this work. She looks for what each one has identified as well-crafted in his own draft. This teacher finds gems. Sometimes she puts a magnifying lens in her miner's light and searches all night for one gem. The many writers in her charge want to know what she will find. As a more senior writer, her findings often surprise them.

Our current ways of trying to teach skills within the context of supportive response evolved when students and teachers revolted against the question of the teacher-corrector: "Which errors will I highlight?"

For years we evaluated papers with this guideline and for years students erred unendingly. With this tremendous emphasis on what the writers needed to do differently, how come students entered successive years of school not able to use apostrophes and not knowing the difference between *your* and *you're*? Maybe we needed to ask a different question: "What skill(s) is this writer purposefully working on?"

I read the writer's self-evaluative note to me and find out where he says I'll find evidence of growth and where I'll find something he's concerned about. I'll read his paper as a teacher, reader, and writer. As his teacher, I'll celebrate his growth, address his worries, and maybe bring up some of my own. As a reader, I expect to learn and enjoy this paper, and as a writer I will look for artistry and craftsmanship. I hope I'll see evidence of some skills I've taught.

From teachers in whose classrooms I have studied, I have distilled three principles they keep in mind when they work with their students on skills.

First, they teach autonomy. Their students learn not to rely on the teacher but rather to evaluate their own work. They learn whom to ask for help or where to go to help themselves. The teachers structure their classrooms so the students can get help when they need it from various sources.

Second, these teachers teach what the students know they need. They spend time with their students when they are in the process of reading and writing. These teachers listen while their students try to solve problems and teach the skills the students need and can handle in order to move ahead.

Third, these teachers make good use of their time. They may have thirty students and maybe a list of ninety skills to teach. That's twenty-seven hundred encounters. Impossible. When a student needs help, the teacher selects the skill most crucial to the text at hand, but she doesn't necessarily teach the skill to only one child. She may gather a group, teach a mini-lesson to the class, or teach a series of mini-lessons. Often a student in the class already knows the skill the writer needs, and that child can teach the one in need. Several children teach and learn a skill on any one day. The teacher teaches the skills the other children in the classroom cannot teach—and that's not many.

There is no standard list of skills to teach for either reading or writing, but many teachers have either their own mental list, a list provided by a company, the school's curriculum guide, or an accountability system. Regardless, skills are a necessary part of any program. Of the many skills on various lists, general categories exist for study skills, usage, punctuation, phonics, spelling, and context clues. My main goal is to show how reading-writing teachers teach these skills to classes of students who evaluate their own messages and need for skills.

Phonics

Phonics competence varies from knowledge of the long *i* sound in *fright* to the *th* digraph. One April, second grader Valerie read a poem to Leslie Houser and stopped at *fright*. The context was sparse and Valerie couldn't guess what this word might be. Because context wouldn't work, her teacher waited for Val to tackle the word phonetically. Leslie had to hear Val's attempt in order to know how to help. Val finally began, "*/fri/.*" She paused and tried again, "*/fri/.*"

Her teacher wrote "fright—short i" in her notes and tried to think of a way to teach this sound. Leslie remembered a book many of the children liked with *night* in the title and asked Val to get it. By the time Val returned, she had already noticed the similarity between *night* and *fright.* She read right on and after the two of them shuddered together in a brief discussion of the poem, Leslie sent Val to partner with Pedro and make a long list of *igh* words. The children had created word families (Johnston 1999) many times, and Leslie watched as they began. She then looked for another child who needed her.

Mostly, the children ask one another for help while they read, but Leslie sets aside time to listen to children read to her as well. She has found that her individual time with them is invaluable (Gill 2000). She constantly evaluates to determine what to teach, teaches, and works alongside the child to ensure the child's forward momentum. Leslie also hears them in small groups and teaches brief lessons there, as well. She could have postponed the *igh* lesson for a group setting, which she often does, depending on how many children need a particular skill.

She becomes aware of many of their needs within their writing. They get most of their phonics practice while they write as they sound out the words they need (Wilde 1997). Leslie knows her students get much more practice with sounding out words than they did three years ago when she did not set aside time for them to write every day. Her rounds among them as they write and read and her sessions with them in small groups keep her informed about their use of phonics skills.

Punctuation

Joshua, a third grader, sat at a table with three classmates as they all wrote. Josh was polishing his draft about getting ready for a football game.

Going to a football game

One dull Sunday morning I got up & went to the breakfast table. Mom Pop & my little sister Jessica were already there. "Good morning I said. "Good morning my father said. How would you like to go to the Oriole's soccer game? "Would 1? I said Yesss! When? We'll go about 2:00. I had never been to an Oriole's game before!

Part II

It was almost 2:00. "I can't wait I can't wait. I kept on saying. My Dad said he had some good news & he had some bad news. "I want to hear the good news first I said. O.K. . . .

Joshua drew boxes around the places he thought needed different punctuation. He drew his first box around the final *g* in his "Good morning" to his family, a second box around the final *g* in his father's reply, another around the *I* when Josh says, "Would I?", a fourth around the final *t* in his second "I can't wait," and his last box around the final *t* in *first* when he says, "I want to hear the good news first."

Joshua opened the book he was reading to find out how the author had punctuated talk, but it was a nonfiction book about soccer and he didn't see conversation. So, he went to the classroom library, opened Miriam Cohen's *Second Grade—Friends Again!*, and found quotation marks. He thought he knew how to punctuate the beginning of conversation, but the closing had confused him, so he hadn't attempted closings when he had drafted. Now, on page 52, he found, "'Okay! Batter up! Nathan, you're first,' said Mr. Zito." Josh studied the comma and quotation marks after *first* and returned to his writing. He fixed his first, second, and fifth boxes, but the question mark after "Would I?" and the periods in his repetition of "I can't wait. I can't wait" confused him.

He went to a friend who said he should put quotation marks in those two places. Joshua did. He was then supposed to ask a classmate to study his entire draft for punctuation possibilities, but Doug Fortin paused at his table, and Joshua requested a conference.

Doug glanced at the five boxes, commented positively on four of them, and said, "The period after 'I can't wait' is supposed to be a comma, just like after the 'Good mornings' and 'good news first.' Periods become commas in quotes."

Next Doug scanned Joshua's "Punctuation I Can Do" list.

Punctuation I Can Do
1. I put capital letters on names of towns.
2. I put capital letters on names of teams.
3. I put capital letters on names of people.
4. I put periods after Mr. and Mrs.
5. I put a period at the end of a story.
6. I put a dash in a score like 23–26.

He scanned Joshua's draft and found he had attended to these skills. Then he quickly read the entire draft, on the lookout for punctuation possibilities. As he did so, he decided to focus on the quotations, since that is what Joshua had done. He quickly helped Joshua locate all the quotes and helped him fix each trouble spot. Doug closed the conference with a mini-lesson for the entire table about ways to close quotes. He moved to another table, on the lookout for a student who had this skill—someone who could help students on future days.

Context Clues

Two third-grade children sat on a pillow in the classroom library and looked at *The Top of the World* (Jenkins 1999), the book Francis Damone had read to them after recess. Other children indulged in various literacy experiences around the room while their teacher made her rounds. As she approached the library, Anna announced, "We can read this!"

"Wow! Will you read some pages to me?" Francis knew this information book was not necessarily an easy read, but it was well-crafted, and the children loved it.

As they started to read, two nearby children came to listen. Before long, the readers got stuck on the word *sacred*. Anna, one of the listeners, said, "Just keep going. You'll get it."

The readers read on, "They consider the mountain *sacred* and won't start up without a Puja, a ceremony to ask the gods for protection and permission to climb."

Anna said, "I know what that word is," and went back and read the sentence.

The readers read the rest of the page.

Francis needed to continue her rounds, but before she left she held a skills conference. "You really like that book, don't you? Why?"

"It's amazing!"

"It's scary!"

"I think so, too. I noticed back here [Francis pointed to *sacred*], you didn't know *sacred* at first. Tell me how you figured it out."

"Anna told us to skip it."

"Yes, she told you to read ahead and then go back. That worked, didn't it? How did you know the word, Anna?"

"I know it from church."

Learning how to use context clues is one of the many strategies readers must acquire in order to become independent (Forsyth & Roller 1997/1998). Readers who are writers are used to pushing onward. When they write, they put down their message as it comes and move ahead. They constantly reread—especially young writers—in order to know what word they want to write next. They have a line of thought going and they want to get it down.

Writers attack reading in a similar fashion. They have a line of thought going and keep it moving. Young children need many familiar books to read so they can try to construct the meaning themselves. They're familiar with the book and have a general idea of what's next. They begin to read the way they begin to write. They jump in fearlessly.

Younger children often read books their teacher has read to the class many, many times. These repetitions help them figure out words in context.

Older students use context skills frequently when they meet unknown words. Often their books contain more helpful contexts than those of younger readers, and sometimes they need to read ahead farther than one sentence. At times, they don't need to return. Every word isn't necessary, and good readers know it is unwise to dwell on every single word.

Study Skills

Sam approached his teacher. He was reading a book about some boys on an adventure and had found a section in which the boys watch some otters. He didn't know for sure what an otter is and there was no picture. His teacher started to tell Sam about the otters at her cabin but bit her tongue. She'd better let Sam try on his own first. Then she'd add her tale. "How can you find out, Sam?"

Without an answer, Sam went off to the library, where he cornered the librarian. "Ms. Taft, help me find out about otters."

Wise Marcia Taft calmly responded, "What are two places you could look, Sam?"

Sam stopped short. He liked videos; maybe he could find one on otters. If not, he would try the Internet.

These adults returned Sam's question to him. They wanted him to be able to say at the end, "I did it myself." Both women helped him find options when he had a question, and he chose the process he would use to find his own answer to his own question.

Sam did not find a video, but he found a picture on the Internet that he shared with both Marcia and an older boy from another class who happened to be in the library. This boy had written a report on beavers and found otters interesting; he said they seemed to be somewhat like beavers. Both boys disappeared around the stacks to find a book. The older boy helped Sam read two paragraphs in a section about otters. When Sam heard "Otters have webbed feet like ducks," he decided instantly he had to read this to his class.

He practiced and practiced the two paragraphs and showed off his study skills two days later when he read to his class. They talked about otters. His teacher related her story about the otters who slide on the icy riverbanks at her cabin in the wintertime. Eventually, one of the students asked Sam, "How did you find those paragraphs?"

"Well, Mark's big brother was in the library and showed me this, the index. Here [pause while Sam flipped pages] is the word *otter* and three page numbers. Sometime when you need some information, I'll show you how it works."

His teacher dated "Knows how to use an index" on Sam's skills list. She also wrote: "Otters. Learned index skill from older boy in library. Will teach others."

This cycle goes on. Children need assistance and their teachers help them help themselves. Their teachers give specific instruction when the children can't move ahead. They learn specific skills when they want to learn meaningful, interesting information.

Spelling

Some writers create perfect drafts on their first try, but most of us don't produce final drafts the first time we compose a piece of writing. We struggle through our message from beginning to end in order to find out just how our facts and feelings come together into some worthwhile information. Then, we go back and work on smaller and smaller chunks until we get down to the one-word level. The main thing students learn about spelling is when to check their words. They learn when spelling counts.

The following examples illustrate the difference between what Scott wrote about his grandma when he drafted without worrying about spelling, and what he might have written if he had worried about spelling from the get go. Here's what he wrote:

> Won da me and my fathr and mothr want to my gramus to vises hr becus she jest came awt ov the hospdl. She had a ne operashun becus hr ne crdlig is bad. Wal we wr thar we toct with ech othr my gramu told us thot hr ne is betr
>
> [One day me and my father and mother went to my grandma's to visit her because she just came out of the hospital. She had a knee operation because her knee cartilage is bad. While we were there we talked with each other. My grandma told us that her knee is better.]

The following is, in general, what I predict Scott would have written if he had worried about spelling on his first draft:

> Me and my dad and mom saw my grandma. She had a bad leg. It is good now.

Effective writing teachers judge the first sample as the better piece of writing and, because we want students to compose interesting material, we do not tell them to spell correctly on their first drafts. Students who worry about spelling too early tend to use familiar words and compose dull pieces of writing.

Further, if students think they are going to have to correct the spelling in every piece of writing, a dislike for what lies ahead may also lead them to curtail their use of interesting words, which limits their thinking and learning. The time they spend fixing the spelling on some so-so drafts is better spent on the creation of a new draft that may turn out to be significant. It is important for writers to write; the writing teacher wants her students to spend a significant portion of their writing time composing. Spelling instruction makes sense in classrooms in which children write and read all the time (Snowball & Bolton 1999).

When a writer decides to bring a piece of writing to final copy, it's time to think about spelling. For very young or inexperienced writers whose writing is to be typed for some type of publication that will be read by others, adults carry much or all of the responsibility for spelling. As soon as his teacher thinks Scott can spell some of his words, she will teach him to change as many of his misspellings as reasonable. When he can take spelling responsibilities as a positive challenge, he will start to take charge of turning his draft into a piece of writing composed with conventionally spelled words.

Typically Scott circled as many as five words he thought he had spelled incorrectly. In the case of his hospital piece he circled *hospdl, operashun,* and *gramu,* three words he had struggled with and was proud of but felt unsure about. Supposedly he could have then found out how to spell those words by looking at previous pieces of his own writing, other children's writing, books, charts in the room, and his own list of "Words I Can Spell" stapled in his writing folder. In Scott's case, his "Words I Can Spell" list consisted of:

me	had
and	a
my	is
to	we
she	with
came	us
the	

Scott, however, didn't attempt to find the spellings of the words he circled. Apparently he had yet to develop these habits. Scott immediately approached a classmate, the supposed second step. His friend knew they could find *hospital* in the telephone book, and finally they did. Scott wrote it at the bottom of his writing. He had learned that erasing and fixing only resulted in rips in his papers.

Scott then decided it was time to go to his teacher. But, before I show what happened in his editing conference, I feel compelled to step back and take a larger look at what was happening.

Ellen Koritz devoted the majority of her time to learning from her children about the information, emotion, and facts in their writing. When a student and she reflected on the instruction she had provided over the course of the year, they both remembered the conversations they had about sport fishing, which is common along the southeastern seacoast, grandmother's new knee, and a report on Louis Pasteur. Mainly, Ellen learned about information and feelings from each writer as the children told her, in various contexts, about the content of their data and emerging drafts. These were the exciting conversations that kept the writers' momentum on high. Scott loved to tell her and the other children at his table about the huge scar on his grandma's knee.

Now, back to the editing conference. Ellen quickly scanned Scott's "Words I Can Spell" list and kept it in mind as she read through his draft. These words were to be spelled correctly, and if he had had trouble with them, she might not have asked him to suggest a new one for his list. On this day he seemed ready for additions and they selected two: *grandma* and *bad.* He selected *grandma* and she suggested *bad.*

She asked, "Who else has written about their grandma?"

Scott thought, "Oh! Cathy!"

"When we're finished, you can ask her about it. Now, it's time for you to learn how to spell *bad.*" She told him to write it next to *had,* as she conducted a brief mini-lesson with him on the similarities between these two words. She wondered if he could think of another word for this pattern and he asked, "Sad?"

"Sure, please write it here."

He did, went to find Cathy, and then entered his piece of writing on the computer for publication. Later, with Ellen at his side, he spell checked it. Spell checking is a helpful skill for the children to learn, but it can be tricky at this age when the spell checker often has no idea what the misspelled word might be. Also, Scott often didn't know which choice was correct, but by the third repetition of *knee,* he corrected it himself. Spell checkers do help us learn to spell. His piece of writing then looked like this:

> Won day me and my father and mother want to my grandmas to vises her because she jest came out of the hospital. She had a knee operation because her knee cartilage is bad. While we were there we talked with each other my grandma told us that her knee is better.

Ellen then perfected it herself at the computer with Scott beside her, and it was ready to print out, one sentence per page, for a book he would illustrate, practice until perfect, and read to the class for response.

In some classrooms I see students, regardless of age, draft on computers, which is excellent. It appears to not matter how old or young we are, many of us prefer to compose on screen. I know preschool children who send e-mail messages.

In classes where students don't have computer access, or in classes of more experienced students, I see teachers use variations of Scott's conference with Ellen. As the teacher reads through the draft, if she finds misspellings of any kind, she indicates them with a soft pencil mark in the margin and says, "There's a word for you to check somewhere in these two lines." If the draft is full of misspellings, the teacher does this with some and corrects the rest herself. Mainly, the teacher is careful to not overwhelm the writer with corrections.

On any given day, some students are editing their work, others are reading, and some are in the midst of drafts that may go on for days. The varying work speeds of the students save the teacher. As she moves about the room during workshop, they need her for different reasons.

When Ellen finished with Scott, she walked to another section of the room, and Eric asked her, "How do you spell *lean*?" He was just catching on to the notion of sound-symbol correspondences and really wanted to know which letters went with the sounds he heard. Ellen had to be careful. If someone told him how to spell a word, he wouldn't practice the new phonics skills he was just acquiring (Strickland 1998). So when Eric asked how to spell *lean*, Ellen answered, "What do you mean?"

"I *lean* over when I jump."

"Oh, yes, you do, don't you? Say *lean*."

"*Lean*."

"Yes. Say it again and listen to the way it starts."

"*Lean*, /l-l-l/ *L*?"

"How do you make an *L*?"

Eric didn't respond.

Ellen asked, "Who could help you?"

"Denise."

Even though Eric was right in the middle of composing, he went to Denise. Young children often demand help with spelling while they are composing initial drafts because their command of phonics is so limited, they can't even get their ideas down. Eric's teacher taught him to get help from other children when he needed it. She did not provide help that another child in the class could provide, but she did help Eric think through the process that enabled him to realize what help he needed and whom he could ask.

Usage

Marcel, a fifth grader, had decided to publish his final draft about when the police stopped him on his dirt bike. He thought it was flawless. No edits necessary.

Darcy Raynor began by checking through Marcel's portfolio to find his goal, plan, and proposed documentation. His goal was to "Write like a journalist and publish an article in the fifth-grade newsletter." His plan was to "Write about my dirt bike experience, read my draft to my family to find out what they think, read it to Ricardo, read it to a girl, and make a final draft if I need to." His documentation plan was to put a copy of the newsletter in his portfolio with a reflection. Darcy had asked Marcel for an update on how things were going more than once while he was working on this draft, and now she read it with the newsletter in mind. His portfolio served as her guide.

One of his entries was his "Things I Can Do in Writing" list and she quickly scanned it before she read his article:

Things I Can Do in Writing
1. I capitalize names, towns, and states.
2. I put periods after abbreviations.
3. I use were with plurals.
4. I know to, too, and two.

As Darcy carefully read his article she noticed that Marcel had forgotten a period after one abbreviation and said, "You and David found almost everything, but check the second one again." Marcel found the spot, inserted a period, and placed a mark in the margin of his printout so he could find it when he returned to the computer.

Darcy noticed one usage error and didn't think the correction would confuse Marcel. The decision about whether a usage pattern should be corrected is often difficult, because usage in writing usually reflects oral language patterns. A young child often cannot imitate adult language patterns he does not yet use, and if the teacher corrects the child's words with too much precision, the child sometimes can't read the corrected piece. For older children, their confidence is shaken if their writing is overcorrected. Darcy had learned to be careful about usage. Standard English is sometimes very foreign.

One sentence in Marcel's draft read: "Me and my friend went to the sand dunes." They opened the book he was reading at the time and looked for three similar constructions. This took two minutes, with the help of two of his nearby friends. Marcel recorded "My friend and I" on his "Things I Can Do" list, dated the entry, indicated the necessary correction in the margin, and went to the computer lab to make his final corrections.

Hmmmm . . .

Everything I've mentioned here sounds smoother and easier than it is in real life. The teaching of skills is one of the hardest parts of teaching writing. And we worry so much about it. Knowing which skills to teach to whom, how, and when can seem very complicated.

The *when* may give us the most problems. Now that we try to teach writing from the students' drafts, our own, and the writing of professionals, rather than from textbooks, we tend to miss the sequential exercises provided by numbered pages, worksheets, and workbooks. It's so easy to forget how simple those worksheets were for some students (to do them wasted their time), how impossible they were for others (to do them wasted their time), and how perfect they were for not nearly enough students.

We also tend to forget how poorly constructed some of those worksheets and pages were. Sometimes students who knew a skill couldn't understand the workbook page, and they became the wronged owners of low scores.

Reasonably often a student could do a page but didn't seem to bring those exercises to the front of his mind when he wrote. It's tough for students to transfer an exercise on commas in a series to their own writing. It's our profession's awareness of the necessity of teaching skills in context that brought about many of the big changes in writing instruction. When we help a student punctuate the very draft on his desk in order to make it say what he wants it to say, those funny little marks take on significance.

To be on the spot at just this right moment seems nearly impossible. However, when students write every day and we spend our time among them, we do help some every day. And, we know who knows which skills so we don't have to address every need we meet. We refer students to others. When one problem keeps coming up over and over, we teach a group or the class.

In the midst of this daily, diverse writing, it is likely that the skills designated for a grade level will all arise. If not, maybe they are erroneously on the list. Or we could introduce a few within our own writing and talk to the students about their need to include them in their work. The use of semicolons may not come up naturally, but when students probe their drafts for places where they could use them, these handy marks can become part of their repertoires.

The study of literature often brings many interesting uses of skills to students' attention, and they love searching for pages where authors use and diverge from rules. Donald Hall's sentence formations on page 25 in *The Man Who Lived Alone* (1984) can bring forth lively conversations about this nonconventional man and the author's uses of nonconventional structures to portray him:

> Sometimes in the winter he would eat
> tomatoes out of his Ball jars three times a day.
> Sometimes peas.
> Sometimes applesauce.
> Sometimes he would buy a case of cornflakes or one of graham
> crackers and eat nothing else until he finished the case.

Processes Readers and Writers Use

Fourteen

My dad reigns as the prime storyteller in my life. He definitely makes sense of his world as he relives it. A few days ago he told me a string of stories that started with a graduation taking place the following Friday, segued into an incident that occurred when he was in second grade in 1921, meandered through other anecdotes involving torn collars and overalls, and ended up with his cousin Hilda's phone call in December of 1999. She had said, "You've always been my favorite cousin."

His string of stories showed him as a nonviolent person and when this stance had caused him problems, but Reno Mauseth is the only person who pushed Dad over the edge. He is the only person Dad ever hit, and that was in March of 1922 "on the corner north of Alden, Minnesota, where you turned to go north to grandma and grandpa's farm. Reno and I became friends later and were all through our adult life. He's gone now, you know."

Never once in this twenty-five-minute chain of stories did Dad tell me the overall meaning of this set of reflections. As he reviewed this strand of his life it was up to me to figure out how all those stories fit together. I did, as best I could.

At eighty-six he is trying to figure out who he is. Actually, he probably knows, but he is trying to convince himself that he has been and still is a good person. He probably knows that, also, but he's trying to figure out how he evolved. It's time for him to be at peace with who he is and the experiences that formed Harry. He could have made different decisions at many intersections. He wonders if he made the right ones.

Readers and Writers Search for Significance

My dad never has a problem thinking of a story to tell; any comment by someone else can trigger a story within him. That story then becomes the starting point for another and another as a puzzle within one leads him forward. When storytellers, writers, and readers find a truth to pursue, the meaning they find within a task tends to become clearer as they become more deeply involved. The meaning of a book takes shape, or a draft gains a sharper focus.

Frieda's self-assigned writing task was to write a letter to the city council. She thought a bikeway on her street would help her and other upper-elementary students ride more safely than they then did. Frieda believed the street was wide enough for the city to paint a narrow lane down both sides, and she intended to write to the council about this. She called city hall to find out how to address her envelope. The secretary, evidently interested in this relatively young citizen, gave Frieda some news. When she returned to the classroom from making her phone call, Frieda said, "I didn't know someone was trying to convince the city council to add a bikeway to Chestnut Street. Maybe I can work with her. That sounds better than to work on my idea," which was to convince the council to add a bikeway to Ash Street, two blocks over. So, Frieda changed her goal slightly.

Frieda called the woman who wanted the bike lane on Chestnut, and the woman said she was planning to attend a council meeting. She asked Frieda, "Would you like to go?" Would she! Before the meeting, Frieda created a plan to find out about the council members. She read any information she could find in the daily paper about them and learned what each one stood for. She knew who would likely support the bikeway and who might not.

Finally, the date of the council meeting arrived. Frieda, the woman who wanted the bikeway, and a third person attended, and Frieda saw the audience for her letter in person. Later, she and her new partner drafted a careful letter. On the day Frieda read it to the class, this helpful adult came to the classroom.

This authentic writing task, the real audience, and the significant purpose all merged to create a unique writing process for Frieda. When the learning processes that writers and readers follow remain open, opportunities emerge. Explorers use every process they can think of to get from A to Z. There is no prescribed process to follow. The writing process is the one a writer uses for a particular task, and it evolves.

In order to find significance in the book *River, Cross My Heart*, by Breena Clarke (1999), I repeatedly asked myself this question while I read: "What is this book about?" When I started to read it, I simply did so because it was the book my book group chose for January. By the time I finished, I realized it showed, for me, the necessity of telling one's story. Johnnie Mae had to tell hers in order to find any sense in her sister's drowning. In addition I talked about it with my husband. His questions helped me think even more carefully about what the book meant, and I wanted my own thoughts to be clear before I attended the group.

Often, I don't have a clear notion until my group talks about a book. Upon occasion, I look up some additional information to help me determine the significance of a book. Friends of mine draw to help them find their own meaning in a tome. In our group, some members keep a journal and read from it at our meetings. Some bring news clippings of related incidents. The various ways we use to search for significance helped us talk about *River, Cross My Heart.*

No one else in my ten-person book group appeared to find the same significance in Johnnie Mae's telling of her tale as I did. Our discussion about racial strife and Georgetown added layers of meaning to my single thought. I joined this group because I wanted others to enlarge my thinking, and they have.

I took notice of Patrick Shannon's (2000) arguments when he wrote about the *New York Times* article in which a reporter related this data: 25 percent of the fourth graders in the poorer neighborhoods of New York state failed the state test of reading and writing. However, while giving various reasons for what works and doesn't in reading and writing instruction, the significance of these test scores, as seen by Shannon, went by the wayside. "No one interviewed in the *Times* article even touched on the possibility that the New York test indicates . . . much about the society in which Americans live" (396).

Louise Rosenblatt, interviewed by Nicholas Karolides (1999), said, "more important than anything else right now is the political situation. . . . My belief in the importance of the schools in a democracy has . . . increased over the years" (169). When she started to write in 1938, outside forces threatened us, but now she worries about inside forces with similar, narrow minds. She encourages us to create classrooms in which we seek value in everyone's "reservoir of past experiences in order to create personally significant new meanings" (167).

We skirt issues all the time. Moffett (1992) advises teachers to promote their students' growth toward a set of values in which they care not only about content and themselves but for the welfare of one another. In so doing we may find significance in our work as readers and writers.

Readers and Writers
Pursue Options

Liberating readers and writers—teaching them various options they might choose among as they move forward—thrills students and teachers. Before the thrill, however, teachers feel genuine fear: mayhem will ensue. To offer students options is to take a humongous step into the unknown. Not telling students what to write and how to do it goes against the grain of writing teachers who are not writers and readers, but those who do write and read feel the necessity of choice. They feel it in their guts. They know from their own experiences.

Some learners dig deep within to try to understand a long-buried stance and some research a newly found question, such as "What is dengue fever?" Regardless, they have their computers turned on at all times. Writers and readers never know when something they've always wondered about will resurface, or when something new will pique their interest. They're ready to write and consider options throughout every day as they live their lives.

This behavior of writers confuses the world of education and leads to large misunderstandings. Many persons don't know how to evaluate writers when they all write something different. These educators worry about how to score writing if one student writes a personal narrative about his torn overalls, one writes a travel brochure about dengue fever, and another writes a song about a hike in the Blue Ridge Mountains. Many educators fret about who should receive a 4 and who a 3. Oftentimes, to avoid the complexity this diversity begets, evaluators assign everyone the same topic.

Then, the dominoes start to fall. Anxious for their students to perform well, teachers assign topics to students as preparation for the tests, which could be wise. Unfortunately, many educators, *very* eager for their students to perform well, assign topics to their students all year. Their students struggle to become writers. Many, under careful direction, can find passionate interests within assigned topics, but it is hard for these students to plan ahead, to be on the lookout for what they want to write about, to be excited about the possibilities they might explore. Even with leeway within assigned topics, writers who write only to someone else's topics can't develop the mindset of a writer who is always on the alert for ideas to explore via drafts.

Even writers who do know it is their own responsibility to find something to write about have difficulties at times. Novelists sometimes take a break between books. They may need a rest. They may read while they think about what to pursue next. An intense writing project takes lots of energy and the writer knows she must be enthused about it. During this break from writing, she reads, gathers experiences, jots connections in her journal, reflects, talks, and considers options. She may write several small pieces as fillers, and they may even be significant. A poem for mother's birthday, and a funny pop-up book might precede the well-researched letter about the advisability of the new traffic lights on First and Chestnut.

In an effort to honor this desire of many writers and readers—their desire to pursue a passion and come forth in a public way with an opinion—our profession has sought and found ways to value diverse writers (Sunstein & Lovell 2000). States no longer need to assign topics or genres. In the meantime, while our profession goes through the process of moving away from unidimensional tests, students must not spend entire years writing essays on assigned topics. In order for a writer to write an effective essay on an assigned topic, writers need diverse writing experiences. When a student writes a poem and her teacher helps her see the strengths of exact word choice in it and in poems of professionals, this young writer can use that skill when she writes her essay. There is tremendous crossover among genres.

In an effort to ensure diversity in reading and writing instruction in the classrooms of New Hampshire, the state department of education published an addendum to our state frameworks. In the addendum, classroom vignettes written by teachers, including some of us at the university level, show scenes in which students write, interact, and read from many sources at any one time. At the end of each classroom scene, we list the various proficiencies from the state framework the children worked on in that scene.

For example, Ellen Phillips (1997) wrote about a first-grade class who started to study bears when one student's grandma saw one near her bird feeder on a Saturday night. The children wrote a letter to the local paper to ask people who had seen bears to call them so they could ask them questions. They read factual information, fiction, and poems in books and magazines. They invited Mr. Evans, the town fish and game warden, to come to their class. They surveyed the school to find out if anybody had seen a bear.

One student drew a simple map of the town on which he pasted cut-out bears where residents had seen them. A group of three created a chart to show information about brown and black bears. Some students created illustrated pieces of writing. The children considered many options throughout their study.

Of the eleven proficiencies listed at the end of this vignette, four are:

- Students should be able to identify a specific purpose for their reading such as learning, locating information, or enjoyment. (Reading)
- Students should understand that different purposes require different formats and styles of writing. (Writing)
- Students should listen effectively to spoken and audio-visual message s including stories, factual presentations, and directions. (Speaking, listening, and viewing)

■ Students should use language for a variety of purposes such as sharing information. (English language uses)

In the introduction to this document we explained the advantages of complex classrooms:

> The purpose of these vignettes is to show ways that teachers can help their students meet the proficiencies in the New Hampshire language arts framework within rich classroom environments. The State Department of Education sees students' involvement as a key to their academic accomplishments. . . .
>
> Each scene brings together many proficiencies, which strengthens the children's learning more so than if the teacher provides isolated learning experiences for each proficiency. If the teacher does that, the children will have to bring these strategies together on their own when they need these skills in their daily lives. . . .
>
> What we want is for students to know how to listen to each other, talk to each other, write in a sensible way, and read with understanding—all interrelated acts. We create classrooms in which children practice all these proficiencies simultaneously.

The teachers in this addendum booklet all create unique classrooms. One size cannot fit all (Cambourne 2000). Some place a great deal of emphasis on response to literature; one brings math, social studies, and literature together via time lines; and others use environmental studies as a central focus. All resound with the voices of teachers and students who flourish when they hike their own paths.

Readers and Writers Purposefully Grow

Karen Boettcher, a sixth-grade teacher in Manchester, purposefully changes her instructional processes in her lifelong effort to create a classroom in which her students want to become better readers and writers. She experienced a transformative moment when Artie, one of her students, startled her. As a writing teacher, Karen had learned to write supportive comments on students' drafts, rather than comments they would perceive as criticisms of their efforts. Only two months prior to the incident with Artie, she had changed from a basal-based to a writing-based reading program, and she had not yet become very skilled at writing responses to her students.

Karen had started a system in which her students each wrote a brief statement at the end of each reading period about whatever they had read that day, but after the third day of doing this, when she read their journals, she found dry comments like "I liked the story," and "The book is pretty interesting." Karen wrote a comment after each student's third entry.

"Be more specific" was something she frequently wrote.

The comments they wrote after her nudges included more specifics, such as Lynne's "Duncan was a bully. He stole lunches and was being mean to the Tartan."

In Artie's log, after his brief, nondescript entry, Karen wrote, "Why?" Artie responded to this nudge differently than any other student. He blackened it out! Then, however, he did write an elaborate comment.

Artie's decision to blacken out her comment bothered Karen a great deal. She asked, "Should I be writing comments? In this project we are supposed to be focusing on the students' evaluations." Somehow, Karen wanted to place her students in a position where they would find it valuable to write comments about their day's reading. Her overriding purpose was for her students to find value in their work; this drove all her curricular decisions. She talked to them about this and they decided to bring their logs to their groups upon occasion and read significant comments aloud as conversation starters.

Karen reflected, more so than in previous years of her career, on many of her actions (Hansen 1998a). She used these reflections to guide her own growth as a teacher, and she did not have specific guidelines to follow. She determined what instructional processes she would try in line with her overall purpose and used professional literature, conversations with me, and interactions with her colleagues at our research team meetings to help her.

Similarly, students purposely consider processes to use to promote their own growth. When one student brings a concern to a group, such as this teacher did, others brainstorm. No process of teaching or learning is golden. The student or teacher chooses a way to solve her dilemma and proceeds. During these discussions, others sometimes hear of processes they have never tried. They are ever on the lookout for better ways to do things.

When a child in Pat McLure's primary classroom experimented with and created a pop-up character, lots of students did so. Characters in stories became more lively. More precise action verbs appeared. Writing improved. The students' overall plan was to create "better" stories, and they decided pop-up pages were better than flat ones. These writers purposefully grew (Hansen 1998c) as they considered the effectiveness of various strategies their classmates and professional writers used.

Hmmmm . . .

The careful response process Karen Harris Baroody taught her resource room students enabled them to flourish, and they knew it. They read to one another, and while someone read, the other(s) listened carefully for new information so they could tell the reader what they had learned. They knew they always had to say something when the reader finished, and they couldn't say, "I learned a lot!" They had to quote from what the writer/reader read. They learned to do this, and their perceptions of themselves as learners started to change. Regularly hearing, "This is what I learned from you . . ." made an impact. Their shaky selves started to gain confidence.

Before long, they wanted to read their writing to their regular classes. When Matt did, his draft included pictures of a recent family outing to Ruggles Mine. When he finished he said to his class, "Comments or questions, please." This was not a classroom in which students responded to one another's work, and they didn't know how to react to their classmate.

Scott, another resource room student in this classroom, noted the lull and raised his hand to get the class rolling. He commented that he had learned how heavy pickaxes are. Matt responded by telling them the exact weight and then continued, "Other questions or comments, please."

The adults—his classroom teacher and an assistant—were floored by Matt's ability to take charge of his own sharing session. The resource room environment had affected changes in his ability to see possibilities for himself and in his relationships with others—in the resource room, in his regular classroom, and, ultimately, on the playground.

"These children recognize their abilities and do not limit themselves," wrote Karen for one of our research team meetings. They thought they could write about anything and knew their writing was good enough to share beyond the resource room. Their ability to respond impressed even their teacher. They could tell you exactly what they had learned from their classmates' drafts and what they had learned when they wrote their own. The response system—the evaluation system—promoted their growth.

Momentum

I recently spent four weeks in Itapajé, a town in the mountains of Ceará, a state in the northeast of Brazil. While there, I observed in many classrooms, loved the students who tried desperately hard to teach Portuguese to me, and taught a course on *evaluation and instruction in writing* for forty-five K–8 teachers. We met for four Fridays and Saturdays from 9 A.M. to 6 P.M. During these wonderfully long, full days we wrote, read, listened, talked, laughed, cried, and ate mangoes, beans and rice, and tapioca.

I found it relatively easy to generate excitement for writing; the teachers wrote fascinating drafts. I worried, however, that it would be difficult for them to keep their momentum alive after our course ended. It is much more difficult to keep writing alive than to give birth to it—and that is not easy. To actually be a writer—a person who writes, someone who becomes energized when a pen loops across paper or when letters appear on a screen—remains difficult for many of us.

Luizinha Braga, the superintendent for the K–8 district of Itapajé, enrolled as a student in my class. She wrote, laughed, frowned, and got off task as often as anyone. Ultimately, as she felt the power of our large circle of writers, she and others took on the challenge of creating an ongoing system that would support these teachers and encourage writing throughout the district. Luizinha announced the plan during the afternoon of our last day.

Thirty-nine volunteers from the course would each serve as a mentor to six to ten teachers in the district, which has a total of about 300 teachers. So, everyone would be invited into this change process. The mentors would visit the classrooms of each teacher in her group and vice versa. Each teacher and mentor would identify at least one instructional process each of them did well and one area each of them wanted to improve in her or his teaching. As the teachers set their goals for change, they would pair themselves (facilitated by their mentor, who would have visited each of their classrooms) with someone whose teaching skills complemented theirs. In this way, the various groups of six to ten teachers, under the supervision of a mentor, would help one another work toward their own goals.

In addition, each mentor would convene a monthly study group, at which time they would talk about their students' successes and struggles and review professional articles. Some of these articles would be from professional publications and others the mentors and teachers would write as narratives about their own students, with pedagogical implications. The mentors and teachers would document their growth by creating ongoing portfolios they would bring to each meeting.

An outside consultant, Francisco Cavalcante Jr., would meet with the mentors twice each semester. It sounded like it would work.

The teachers have begun. In one of the classrooms I visited, the little children pursued various literacy tasks, including painting. Later, when some of the children shared their work with the class, one little boy told about a memorable event. My English ears couldn't understand a word of his Portuguese tale, but when he finished, I knew something important had transpired. Not only had he sounded excited, but when he stopped talking, his teacher couldn't contain herself. She jumped up, and through various efforts, and one Portuguese word I had acquired, *cascata*, I realized that the blue streak of paint that slid from the upper left to the lower right of his painting was a nearby waterfall he had recently visited.

Without his words to explain his writing, we would not have focused on the blue streak among the various strokes of paint slanted in multiple directions across this paper. His words showed all of us his focus, and we now knew what he valued in this work. Our evaluation could support his efforts, and he knew we loved his *cascata*.

He worked willingly again the next day. It was up to him to think of something to write about and to choose his medium, which may have been paint, or words, or items cut and pasted from magazines or newspapers. He would create a meaningful message, and when he read it to others, he would make sure it made sense. When he read, he wouldn't struggle to decipher a lineup of words that sounded disconnected to him and his listeners.

This child learned to read by telling his news and he assumed others did likewise. When his teacher read to the class, he heard Brazilian folktales and personal narratives from magazines for teachers, written to be read to children. When his teacher created a three-sentence book about one of her personal experiences and read and reread it to the class, he decided to practice it and read it to the class, as well. He had goals for himself as a reader.

His teacher's evaluation system kept him excited about reading and writing. Every day her goal was to help him find value in his efforts and to highlight for him, with specificity, what she appreciated in his work. Creating and maintaining the students' interest in school is a tremendously difficult undertaking for the teachers in this district, where about six thousand of the seven thousand students in grades 1–8 are in grades 1–4. School attendance is not mandatory. The majority leave after grade 4. Most can't read. None have written; writing does not happen in the schools. The students copy from the board into their copybooks. Literally. But, that is changing in Itapajé.

In the United States we don't have their problem—not exactly. Some of our students find it difficult to learn to read, but not so many. Most of our students write. Regardless, our students can't leave school and a relatively large percentage might be successful enough to choose to stay in school, even if they weren't required to do so. Plus, most of our students' families aren't in the position where they need their children to work for income. For the students of Itapajé who can and do stay in school, their teachers' new focus on "What *can* this child do?" will help them feel less defeated than in their old system—a system found worldwide, including in the United States, wherein teachers highlight errors and return children's papers with condemnations of their efforts to learn to read and write.

Instead, the teachers in Itapajé now try to create classroom cultures in which students celebrate their stretches into unknown territory. These learners' forays into new areas may not always meet with success, as the teachers themselves know through their self-evaluations of their efforts to become more skilled as literacy teachers, but commitment reigns. They know their old teaching processes didn't work. Way too many of their students failed. These teachers are determined to try something new.

Maria, a grade 8 math teacher, remains in my mind. During the break of our first morning she asked me, "What will I learn from this writing class that will help me as a math teacher?" Maria was perfectly willing to try new teaching processes, but what? This is the same position students often find themselves in when they want to become better readers and writers. Informed decisions can only come when the learner has a certain amount of knowledge about the various options and knows where to go to find help. Plus, the writer must see trusted colleagues below her with a strong support net.

During the first day of our course, Maria wrote, but she would not read to her small group when I structured that experience. Instead, another teacher in her group read Maria's draft to the others. As I roved among the fifteen groups of three, the laughter from Maria's group drew me to them. I couldn't understand the Portuguese words, but I knew the group loved what Maria had written, and so, as it turned out, did she.

When we met for our fifth and final day, Maria volunteered to read to the entire class! What growth in confidence (Winsor & Hansen 1999). She read her revision of her initial, humorous draft. The others laughed themselves to tears. This funny little lady amazed us and herself.

However, a few hours later, trouble appeared to arise. By this time, the teachers had each created their individual "Plan for My Professional Growth." After they had worked in groups, I asked for volunteers to share their plans with the class. Maria volunteered, and started by reminding us of questions 1 and 2, "What do I do well as a teacher?" and "What have I recently learned as a teacher?" For the second question, Maria gave us this answer: "I learned to write, read it, rewrite, consider response, and respond to others." As the professor, this answer pleased me, of course.

To the third question, "What would I like to learn next as a teacher?" Maria answered, "To learn ways to help the students in one of my math classes find pleasure in writing." This was a specific goal, a feature of goals I had stressed when, as a class, we had used one teacher's plan for a demonstration. In that case I had recommended to the teacher that she choose a goal for only one class because the processes of collecting data and documenting growth are time-consuming.

Maria shifted position in her chair. Something was about to happen. She reminded us of question 4, "What processes might I use to learn how to do this?", and surprised us with her answer, "I don't know. I want help from all of you right now." I glanced around the room and saw some of the teachers lean forward.

Soon one offered a suggestion: "Within each unit, some of them could write about situations in everyday life where the theory can be applied."

"Some students could create problems to illustrate the content."

"Students may be interested in conducting research in which they use math concepts."

"Maybe some would be interested in creating stories where math is involved/needed."

"Literature books include math."

"There's lots of math in the news, especially in sports."

"And in the economics section."

The suggestions continued as Maria wrote notes at a fast pace. Finally she said, "Thank you!" I wondered if she knew of other learning processes to use in addition to asking her colleagues for ideas. I had stressed that they should think of more than one way to go about generating the ideas they wanted, since one may sound good on paper but not give them the great ideas they had hoped for. Maria, however, was on a roll.

She immediately moved on to question 5, "What might I use as documentation to show that my students find pleasure in writing?"

The other teachers quickly gave her ideas: "You could ask them how they feel about writing."

"Use their notebooks as evidence."

"Create your own math portfolio with your impressions of how things are going, share it with them, and get their responses."

The ideas continued and Maria seemed set to move forward as a math teacher who had learned something from this writing class that could help her. These writers did learn from one another. They told one another what they did well in their drafts, they listened to one another talk about their work, and they asked questions. They tried new forms of writing, used writing to help them understand information, and purposefully polished their new skills.

Now they can use these same learning processes to move themselves forward as teachers. Teachers thrive on tips, always looking for ideas to use in their own work. In their mentoring program they will see and hear about one another's classrooms, tell one another what they do well, and ask questions. They will try new teaching processes and thrive on the support of their colleagues.

The momentum in this district continues to build and will not stop as long as the teachers share their ideas with one another and use one another as resources. They strive to create strong voices for themselves, one another, and their students. In so doing, they move forward as professionals.

All of us experience this feeling of accomplishment and competence as we offer our students spaces in which to grow. We see them push back their chairs, walk across the room, and say to a classmate, "May I read this to you?" Their classmates listen with the evaluative ears of readers, and we all celebrate the possibilities of students who intentionally learn.

References

ADA, ALMA FLOR. 1995. *My Name Is María Isabel.* New York: Aladdin.

ALLEN, CAMILLE. 2001. *Multigenre Papers in Fifth Grade.* Portsmouth, NH: Heinemann.

ALLINGTON, RICHARD. 1983. "The Reading Instruction Provided to Readers of Differing Ability." *Elementary School Journal 83:* 548–59.

ALLINGTON, RICHARD L., & PATRICIA M. CUNNINGHAM. 1996. *Schools That Work: Where All Children Read and Write.* New York: HarperCollins College.

BARBIERI, MAUREEN. 1995. *Sounds from the Heart: Learning to Listen to Girls.* Portsmouth, NH: Heinemann.

BAUER, EURYDICE BOUCHEREAU. 1999. "Walking the Tightrope on Diversity." In *Class Actions: Teaching for Social Justice in Elementary and Middle School,* ed. JoBeth Allen, 84–99. New York: Teachers College Press.

BLECHER, SHARON, & KATHY JAFFEE. 1998. *Weaving in the Arts: Widening the Learning Circle.* Portsmouth, NH: Heinemann.

BRIDGES, LOIS. 1997. *Writing as a Way of Knowing.* York, ME: Stenhouse.

BRIDGES, RUBY. 1999. *Through My Eyes.* New York: Scholastic Press.

BROWN, SUE. 1997. "First Graders Write to Discover Mathematics' Relevancy." *Young Children 54* (May): 51–53.

CAMBOURNE, BRIAN. 2000. "Observing Literacy Learning in Elementary Classroms: Nine Years of Classroom Anthropology." *The Reading Teacher 53*(6): 512–15.

CAMERON, JULIA. 1998. *The Right to Write: An Invitation and Initiation into the Writing Life.* New York: Tarcher/Putnam.

CARR, JANINE CHAPPELL. 1996. "Lee's Story: Living with Loss." In *Meeting the Challenges: Stories from Today's Classrooms,* ed. Maureen Barbieri & Carol Tateishi, 23–33. Portsmouth, NH: Heinemann.

CARROLL, JACQUELIN, & CHARLENE NOELANI-KAHUANUI CHRISTENSON. 1995. "Teaching and Learning About Student Goal Setting in a Fifth-Grade Classroom." *Language Arts 72*(1): 42–49.

CHANDLER, KELLY, & THE MAPLETON TEACHER-RESEARCH GROUP. 1999. *Spelling Inquiry: How One Elementary School Caught the Mnemonic Plague.* York, ME: Stenhouse.

CHOI, SOOK NYUL. 1991. *Year of Impossible Goodbyes.* Boston: Houghton Mifflin.

———. 1997. *Yunmi and Halmoni's Trip.* Boston: Houghton Mifflin.

CLARKE, BREENA. 1999. *River, Cross My Heart.* Boston: Little, Brown.

COONEY, BARBARA. 1994. *Only Opal: The Diary of a Young Girl.* New York: Putnam & Grosset.

COOPER, J. CALIFORNIA. 1996. "When Life Begins!" In *Homemade Love,* by J. California Cooper, 61–78. New York: St. Martin's Griffin.

CURTIS, CHRISTOPHER PAUL. 1995. *The Watsons Go to Birmingham—1963.* New York: Delacorte.

DANIEL, PATRICIA. 1996. "A Celebration of Literacy: Nine Reluctant Students and One Determined Teacher." *Language Arts 73:* 420–28.

DAUENHAUER, ANSLEY. 1996. "Sam and Ansley's Story." *The Quarterly of the National Writing Project & the Center for the Study of Writing and Literacy 18:* 5–7.

DEGROAT, JENNIE. 1997. "Navajo Family Literacy." In *Many Families, Many Literacies: An International Declaration of Principles,* ed. Denny Taylor, 112–15. Portsmouth, NH: Heinemann.

DEPAOLA, TOMI. 1989. *The Art Lesson.* New York: Putnam & Grosset.

DESHON, JO ANNE PRYOR. 1997. "Innocent and Not-So-Innocent Contributions to Inequality: Choice, Power, and Insensitivity in a First-Grade Writing Workshop." *Language Arts 74*(1): 12–16.

DICKINSON, DAVID K., & LORI LYMAN DIGISI. 1998. "The Many Rewards of a Literacy-Rich Classroom." *Educational Leadership 55*(6): 23–26.

DUDLEY-MARLING, CURT. 1997. *Living with Uncertaintly: The Messy Reality of Classroom Practice.* Portsmouth, NH: Heinemann.

DUTHIE, CHRISTINE. 1996. *True Stories: Nonfiction Literacy in the Primary Classroom.* York, ME: Stenhouse.

DYSON, ANNE HAAS, WITH THE SAN FRANCISCO EAST BAY TEACHER STUDY GROUP. 1997. *What Difference Does Difference Make? Teacher Reflections on Diversity, Literacy, and the Urban Primary School.* Urbana, IL: NCTE..

FLETCHER, RALPH. 1998. *Spider Boy.* New York: Yearling.

FLORIO-RUANE, SUSAN. 1994. "The Future Teachers' Autobiography Club: Preparing Educators to Support Learning in Culturally Diverse Classrooms." *English Education 26*(1): 52–56.

FORSYTH, SYLVIA, & CATHY ROLLER. 1997/1998. "Helping Children Become Independent Readers." *The Reading Teacher 51*(4): 346–48.

FRAZIER, CHARLES. 1997. *Cold Mountain.* New York: Vintage.

GALLAS, KAREN. 1998. *"Sometimes I Can Be Anything": Power, Gender, and Identity in a Primary Classroom.* New York: Teachers College Press.

GILL, SHARON RUTH. 2000. "Reading with Amy: Teaching and Learning Through Reading Conferences." *The Reading Teacher 53*(March): 500–509.

GRAVES, DONALD. 1994. *A Fresh Look at Writing.* Portsmouth, NH: Heinemann.

———. 1999. *Bring Life into Learning.* Portsmouth, NH: Heinemann.

GRAVES, DONALD, & JANE HANSEN. 1984. "The Author's Chair." *Language Arts 60*(2): 176–87.

HALL, DONALD. 1984. *The Man Who Lived Alone.* Boston: David R. Godine.

HANSEN, JANE. 1987. *When Writers Read.* 1st ed. Portsmouth, NH: Heinemann.

———. 1989. "Anna Evaluates Herself." In *Risk Makers, Risk Takers, Risk Breakers,* ed. JoBeth Allen & Jana Mason. Portsmouth, NH: Heinemann.

———. 1992a. "The Language of Challenge." *Language Arts 69*(2): 100–105.

———. 1992b. "Literacy Portfolios: Helping Students Know Themselves." *Educational Leadership* May: 66–68.

———. 1996a. "Evaluation: The Center of Writing Instruction." *The Reading Teacher 50*(3): 188–95.

———. 1996b. "Teachers Value Their Grandchildren, Poetry, and Sisters." *Voices from the Middle 3*(4): 3–12.

———. 1997. "Student Record Keeping." *School Talk 3* (November): Newsletter of the National Council of Teachers of English Elementary section (nonpaginated).

———. 1998a. "'Evaluation Is All Day, Noticing What Is Happening': Multifaceted Evaluations of Readers." In *Fragile Evidence: A Critique of Reading Assessment,* ed. Sharon Murphy, with Patrick Shannon, Peter Johnston, & Jane Hansen. Mahwah, NJ: Lawrence Erlbaum.

———. 1998b. *When Learners Evaluate.* Portsmouth, NH: Heinemann.

———. 1998c. "Young Writers: The People and Purposes That Influence Their Literacy." In *Literacy for All: Issues in Teaching and Learning,* ed. Jean Osborn & Fran Lehr. New York: Guilford Press.

———. 1999. "My Geography." In *Ordinary Lessons: Girlhoods of the 1950s,* ed. Susan Franzosa, 65–78. New York: Peter Lang.

HANSEN, JANE, & KATHY STALEY. 1996. *Portfolios: Students as Readers, Writers, and Evaluators.* Three-part video series. Portsmouth, NH: Heinemann.

HART, ELVA TREVIÑO. 1999. *Barefoot Heart: Stories of a Migrant Child.* Tempe, AZ: Bilingual.

HARVEY, STEPHANIE. 1998. *Nonfiction Matters: Reading, Writing, and Research in Grades 3–8.* York, ME: Stenhouse.

HAYNES, MELINDA. 1999. *Mother of Pearl.* New York: Hyperion.

HEARD, GEORGIA. 1989. *For the Good of the Earth and the Sun.* Portsmouth, NH: Heinemann.

HESSE, KAREN. 1997. *Out of the Dust.* New York: Scholastic.

HINDLEY, JOANNE. 1996. *In the Company of Children.* York, ME: Stenhouse.

HUBBARD, RUTH SHAGOURY, & BRENDA MILLER POWER. 1999. *Living the Questions: A Guide for Teacher-Researchers.* York, ME: Stenhouse.

INTERNATIONAL READING ASSOCIATION. 1999. *High-Stakes Assessments in Reading: A Position Statement of the International Reading Association.* Newark, DE.

JENKINS, STEVE. 1999. *The Top of the World: Climbing Mount Everest.* Boston: Houghton Mifflin.

JERVIS, KATHY. 1996. *Eyes on the Child: Three Portfolio Stories.* New York: Teachers College Press.

JOHNSON, DINAH. 1999. *Sunday Week.* Illus. Tyrone Geter. New York: Henry Holt.

JOHNSTON, FRANCINE. 1999. "The Timing and Teaching of Word Families." *The Reading Teacher 53*(September): 64–75.

JOHNSTON, PETER. 1997. *Knowing Literacy: Constructive Literacy Assessment.* York, ME: Stenhouse.

KARELITZ, ELLEN BLACKBURN. 1993. *The Author's Chair and Beyond: Language and Literacy in a Primary Classroom.* Portsmouth, NH: Heinemann.

KAROLIDES, NICHOLAS. 1999. "An Interview with Louise M. Rosenblatt." *Language Arts 77*(2): 158–70.

KEENE, ELLIN, & SUSAN ZIMMERMAN. 1997. *Mosaic of Thought: Teaching Comprehension in a Readers' Workshop.* Portsmouth, NH: Heinemann.

KHANGA, YELENA. 1992. *Soul to Soul: A Black Russian Jewish Woman's Search for Her Roots.* New York: W. W. Norton.

KIRKLAND, JOLEIGH. 1997. "Trust the Students." *Primary Voices K–6 5*(4): 44–45.

LADSON-BILLINGS, GLORIA. 1994. *The Dreamkeepers: Successful Teachers of African American Children.* San Francisco: Jossey-Bass.

LENSKI, SUSAN DAVIS, MARSHA RISS, & GAYLE FLICKINGER. 1996. "Honoring Student Self-Evaluation in the Classroom Community." *Primary Voices K–6 4*(2): 24–32.

LINDFORS, JUDITH WELLS. 1999. *Children's Inquiry: Using Language to Make Sense of the World.* New York: Teachers College Press & Urbana, IL: NCTE.

LOWRY, LOIS. 1993. *The Giver.* Boston: Houghton Mifflin.

MACAULEY, ROBIE, & GEORGE LANNING. 1987. *Technique in Fiction: Revised and Updated for a New Generation.* 2nd ed. New York: St. Martin's.

MADIGAN, DAN, & VICTORIA T. KOIVU-RYBICKI. 1997. *The Writing Lives of Children.* York, ME: Stenhouse.

MARTIN, JACQUELINE BRIGGS. 1998. *Snowflake Bentley.* Illus. Mary Azarian. Boston: Houghton Mifflin.

MCCULLY, EMILY ARNOLD. 1996. *The Bobbin Girl.* New York: Penguin Putnam.

MEEHAN, PAT. 1997/1998. "Beyond a Chocolate Crunch Bar: A Teacher Examines Her Philosophy of Teaching Reading." *The Reading Teacher* 51(4): 314–23.

MILLS, HEIDI, TIMOTHY O'KEEFE, & DAVID WHITIN. 1996. *Mathematics in the Making: Authoring Ideas in Primary Classrooms.* Portsmouth, NH: Heinemann.

MOFFETT, JAMES. 1992. *Detecting Growth in Language.* Portsmouth, NH: Heinemann.

MURRAY, DONALD. 1999. *Write to Learn.* 6th ed. Fort Worth, TX: Harcourt Brace.

NATIONAL COUNCIL OF TEACHERS OF ENGLISH (NCTE). 1998. *Evaluation Matters: What's It All About?* Video. Urbana, IL: NCTE.

———. 1999. *The Limitations of Standardized Tests: A Resolution of the National Council of Teachers of English.* Urbana, IL: NCTE.

NEWKIRK, THOMAS, & PATRICIA MCLURE. 1996. "Telling Stories." In *Language Development: A Reader for Teachers,* ed. Brenda Miller Power & Ruth Shagoury Hubbard. Englewood Cliffs, NJ: Merrill.

OSTROW, JILL. 1998. "I'm Not Sittin' by No Girl!" In *"We Want to Be Known": Learning from Adolescent Girls,* ed. Ruth Hubbard, Maureen Barbieri, & Benda Power, 45–52. York, ME: Stenhouse.

PANTANO, JULIE. 1999. *At the Heart of It: Middle School Writers Use Talk and Multi-Media Journals to Forge a Literate Classroom Community.* Ph.D. dissertation. Durham, NH: University of New Hampshire.

PARK, FRANCES, & GINGER PARK. 1998. *My Freedom Trip: A Child's Escape from North Korea.* Illus. Debra Reid Jenkins. Honesdale, PA: Boyds Mills.

PARKER, DIANE. 1997. *Jamie: A Literacy Story.* York, ME: Stenhouse.

PERFECT, KATHY A. 1999. "Rhyme and Reason: Poetry for the Heart and Head." *The Reading Teacher* 52(7): 728–37.

PHINNEY, MARGARET YATSEVITCH. 1998. "Children 'Writing Themselves': A Glimpse at the Underbelly." *Language Arts* 75(1): 19–27.

ROBERTS, WILLO DAVIS. 1991. *The Girl with the Silver Eyes.* New York: Scholastic.

ROGOVIN, PAULA. 1998. *Classroom Interviews: A World of Knowing.* Portsmouth, NH: Heinemann.

ROLLER, CATHY. 1996. *Variability, Not Disability: Struggling Readers in a Workshop Classroom.* Newark, DE: IRA.

ROMANO, TOM. 1995. *Writing with Passion: Life Stories, Multiple Genres.* Portsmouth, NH: Heinemann.

———. 2000. *Blending Genre, Altering Style: Writing Multigenre Papers.* Portsmouth, NH: Boynton/Cook.

ROWLING, J. K. 1998. *Harry Potter and the Sorcerer's Stone.* New York: Scholastic.

SAAVEDRA, ELIZABETH R. 1999. "Transformative Learning Through a Study Group." In *Making Justice Our Project,* ed. Carole Edelsky, 303–15. Urbana, IL: National Council of Teachers of English.

SAEZ, SHARON. 1995. "Remembering His Shoes and Hat: The Standard of Memory." *Voices from the Middle 2*(1): 42–44.

SCHIRO, MICHAEL. 1997. *Integrating Children's Literature and Mathematics in the Classroom: Children as Meaning Makers, Problem Solvers, and Literary Critics.* New York: Teachers College Press.

SCHWARTZ, STACY. 2000. "My Family's Story: Discovering History at Home." *Social Studies and the Young Learner 12*(January/February): 6–9.

SHANNON, PATRICK. 2000. "We Gotta Get Out of This Place: The Politics of What Works." *The Reading Teacher 53*(5): 394–396.

SMITH, AMY. 2000. "Reflective Portfolios: Preschool Possibilities." *Childhood Education 76*(4): 204–208.

SNOWBALL, DIANE, & FAYE BOLTON. 1999. *Spelling K–8, Planning and Teaching.* York, ME: Stenhouse.

STANDARDS FOR THE ENGLISH LANGUAGE ARTS. 1996. Urbana, IL: NCTE & Newark, DE: IRA.

STIRES, SUSAN. 2000. "To Sit Beside: Learning to Evaluate Reading and Writing." In *The Portfolio Standard: How Students Can Show Us What They Know and Are Able to Do,* ed. Bonnie S. Sunstein & Jonathan H. Lovell, 46–61. Portsmouth, NH: Heinemann.

STRICKLAND, DOROTHY. 1998. *Teaching Phonics Today: A Primer for Educators.* Newark, DE: IRA.

SUNSTEIN, BONNIE S., & JONATHAN H. LOVELL, ED. 2000. *The Portfolio Standard: How Students Can Show Us What They Know and Are Able to Do.* Portsmouth, NH: Heinemann.

TANNER, LAUREL N. 1997. *Dewey's Laboratory School: Lessons for Today.* New York: Teachers College Press.

TAYLOR, DENNY, DEBBIE COUGHLIN, & JOANNA MORASCO, ED. 1997. *Teaching and Advocacy.* York, ME: Stenhouse.

TCHANA, KATRIN HYMAN, & LOUISE TCHANA PAMI. 1997. *Oh, No, Toto!* Illus. Colin Bootman. New York: Scholastic.

TRAFTON, PAUL, & CHRISTINA HARTMAN. 1997. "Developing Number Sense and Computational Strategies in Problem-Centered Classrooms." *Teaching Children Mathematics 4*(December): 230–33.

VON DRAS, JOAN. 1995. "Will the Real Teacher Please Stand Up?" *Primary Voices K–6 3*(1): 30–37.

VOSS, MARGARET. 1996. *Hidden Literacies: Children Learning at Home and at School.* Portsmouth, NH: Heinemann.

WANSART, WILLIAM. 1998. "The Student with Learning Disabilities in a Writing Process Classroom: A Case Study." *Journal of Reading, Writing, and Learning Disabilities International 4*: 311–19.

WHITIN, PHYLLIS, & DAVID WHITIN. 2000. *Math Is Language Too: Writing and Talking in the Mathematics Classroom.* Urbana, IL: NCTE.

WILCOX, CAROL. 1995. "Evaluation: Making Room for Robbie." In *All That Matters: What Is It We Value in School and Beyond?* ed. Linda Rief & Maureen Barbieri, 93–107. Portsmouth, NH: Heinemann.

WILDE, SANDRA. 1997. *What's a Schwa Sound Anyway? A Holistic Guide to Phonetics, Phonics, and Spelling.* Portsmouth, NH: Heinemann.

WINSOR, PAMELA J. T., & JANE HANSEN. 1999. "Coming to Know: Learning Together in Belize." *The Reading Teacher* 52(8): 810–18.

Index